Unity in the Dark

DONALD GILLIES, MA

'Stand fast therefore in the liberty wherewith Christ hath made us free, and be not entangled again with the yoke of bondage' [Gal. 5:1]

The Banner of Truth Trust
78b Chiltern Street, London, W1

First published February 1964
Second impression July 1964

Acknowledgments are due to S.C.M. Press for kind permission to quote from *New Delhi Report*, edited by W. A. Visser 't Hooft, *Despatch from New Delhi* by Kenneth Slack, and *The Hard Facts of Unity* by John Lawrence; and to the Rev. A. T. Houghton for kind permission to quote from his booklet, *What of New Delhi?*

This book is set in 11 on 12 point Times
and printed and bound in Great Britain by
Billing and Sons Limited, Guildford and London

Contents

Contents

1: The challenge

THE ECUMENICAL MOVEMENT CHALLENGES US ON two fronts – thought and action. It is inspired by a lofty ideal and encouraged by a remarkable achievement. It has vision and enthusiasm which shame much of our evangelicalism, stricken by the blight of negative criticism and internecine strife. Ecumenical hope and imagination is a challenge to evangelical despondency and stagnation in a changing world.

What is the Ecumenical Movement? The terms 'ecumenical' and 'ecumenism' are derived from the Greek word which means 'the inhabited world'. It is translated 'all the world' in the Authorized Version of the New Testament.[1] 'Ecumenical' is used in the sense of 'belonging to the whole Christian Church'. It is thus applied to the great Councils of the early Church. In the Roman Catholic Church a council is held to be ecumenical when it has been summoned from the Church throughout the world by the authority of the Pope. The modern Ecumenical Movement is the attempt to bring about Christian unity in the world today, and to recover, on a world-wide scale, the original outward unity of the Church. It aims at the destruction of all divisions within the Church, which is to become one world-wide Christian fellowship.

The movement may be said to have had its inception at the World Missionary Conference in Edinburgh in 1910. This was followed by other conferences on matters of Faith and Order attended by Church leaders from all over

[1] E.g. Matt. 24:14; Luke 2:1; Acts 11:28.

the world. The growing desire for a greater measure of unity among the Churches eventually led to the inauguration of the World Council of Churches in Amsterdam in 1948. This was followed by the second Assembly of the W.C.C. in Evanston in 1954, and the third in New Delhi in 1961. For the purpose of this study, the W.C.C. is regarded as the visible expression and mouthpiece of ecumenism. Unity is now a regular item of discussion in all Church Conferences and Assemblies, in sermon and newspaper, on radio and television, and in ordinary conversation. It was of sufficient interest and importance to form the subject of a memorable debate in the House of Lords on 10 May 1961.

According to ecumenism we must cease to speak of our *unhappy* Church divisions. We must rather regard them as *sinful* divisions. Denominationalism is not a painful necessity, it is a sin. Drastic action is therefore demanded on the part of the Churches to remove our divisions. Disunity is sinful and Christians are responsible before God for its disappearance. It is the will of God that we should be one, and in no other way can we effectively proclaim the Gospel to the world. 'The fathers of the Ecumenical Movement knew that there is a fundamental connection between the obligation of the Church to manifest its essential unity and its calling to make disciples of all nations. Archbishop Söderblom declared in 1921: "By our divisions we Christians are an obstacle for our Saviour in His work of Salvation. We make it difficult for men to believe in Him. The unity of Christians is an imperative necessity so that the world may see and recognize the Lord." '[2]

In the course of the debate in the House of Lords the

[2] Dr W. A. Visser 't Hooft, General Secretary of W.C.C., in his Report at New Delhi.

[8]

Bishop of Southwell said: 'There is one sole Church which the New Testament knows. . . . But, for various reasons, geographical, historical, linguistic, political, social, partly, also, genuinely religious, involving fundamental breaches of principle, that Church has been divided and fragmented into what we know today – that is, a number of divided Churches, self-contained and self-justified, each within its own frontier, whose members have for a long time past been engaged in unchurching one another. We inherit that situation. We are not responsible for its being there. But we are, I think, responsible for trying to change it. That can never be done by any easy short cut and, perhaps, only on very deep and costly levels of mutual forgiveness and charity.'[3]

In the ranks of the movement are those who see it as the fulfilment of a great humanitarian ideal. Their interest is largely pragmatic and utilitarian. But others are drawn by what is to all appearances a scriptural and spiritual idealism. They see the movement as giving expression to a new understanding of the relevance of Christ and the Gospel for our day and as providing a new hope for the fulfilment of the Church's missionary obligation. Indeed, for some, ecumenism comes with the force of a twentieth-century reformation.

The success of the movement to date must give its supporters cause for satisfaction. That Eastern Orthodox, Anglo-Catholic, Modernist, Barthian and Evangelical should be able to meet ostensibly as 'Brethren in Christ' is truly a remarkable achievement. The breakdown of denominational pride and prejudice which has for so long been the bane of Christendom must be heartily welcomed. The new spirit of charity and mutual forbearance between

[3] House of Lords Official Report, 10 May 1961, 236.

Churches – even between Protestant and Roman Catholic – is not to be deplored. It is surely a good thing and much to be desired that members of different churches should be able to meet together and talk in a friendly way. Why should not even Protestants and Roman Catholics meet as friends and encourage mutual help in certain situations?

One effect of the Ecumenical Movement has been to focus attention on the weakness of orthodox evangelical thought concerning the nature and unity of the Church. Evangelicals are charged with confining themselves almost entirely to the doctrine of personal salvation and ignoring what God has to say in His Word about the order and discipline of the visible Church and, in words taken from the New Delhi description of unity, its 'corporate life reaching out in witness and service to all'.[4]

In other words, evangelicals may have preached the Word to and for individuals, but they have failed to preach it to and for communities and churches. If this were done, then evangelicals might, as ecumenism has already done, help to bring a new spirit into denominational life and discover that denominations are not so necessary or sacrosanct as they were once thought to be. This might even be the beginning of a real new Reformation in the rediscovery of New Testament principles for a truly united Reformed church.

Evangelicals are challenged with their failure to declare the whole counsel of God. They have been silent on issues

[4] 'The Church is meant to have a corporate life which moves out powerfully to meet the world, to witness before all men to the Lord whose name it bears and, like its Lord, to serve all men in their need.' – *Witness and Service to All*, R. C. Mackie, p. 3. (One of a series of pamphlets published by the British Council of Churches on the New Delhi Statement on Unity, for use in preparation for the British Conference on Faith and Order, 1964.)

relating to the visible church. They have been satisfied with preaching and observing the true unity of believers while accepting the *status quo* of denominational divisions. But ecumenism insists that this is inconsistent and dishonest in the light of Scripture. Our Lord's prayer in John 17, for example, must mean more than an invisible spiritual unity. An invisible spiritual unity, it is agreed, is the primary meaning of New Testament teaching on unity, but is such an inner unity not to be expressed and completed in a visible unity, witnessed by the world? Ecumenists insist that this is demanded by our Lord's prayer for unity so that the world may believe. The world can only be impressed by what it sees. The church then should be directing its efforts towards the formation of a visible corporate unity.

In view of this strong challenge there is one popular line of defence that Evangelicals may be compelled to abandon. This is the attempt *to justify denominational divisions by denominational co-operation.* Such division has been accepted without question so long as members of the different denominations can come together for the preaching of the Gospel and enjoy extra-denominational fellowship. Christian unity is to be found in certain forms of interdenominational work and witness, in the co-operation of different churches in conferences, conventions and campaigns under the banner, 'All one in Christ Jesus'. But however good such co-operation may be, does it go far enough? Is such a unity a satisfactory expression of the Scriptural ideal? Ecumenism says it is not. Dr R. C. Mackie writes: 'Co-operation by itself so often becomes mechanical; it sticks to the shallows; it cannot reach out, and in the end – sometimes mercifully – peters out. The reason is simply that co-operation is not corporate life; it

[11]

is not being a body. If the co-operation of the churches is really to be a step towards the realization – here and now – of the Church, it needs to have before it the vision of unity suggested in the New Delhi paragraph. It needs to submit itself to the growing pains of becoming a body. This is the whole difference between interdenominational co-operation and ecumenical co-operation. The first never means to become anything else than the meeting for certain purposes of separate units held firmly apart by their independent structures. The second is an effort, no matter how feeble and stumbling, to create the pattern of the whole Church out of the given parts. The one form of co-operation is entered into with a severely limited notion of what is right and practicable to accomplish; the other is entered into with a sense of beginning to make something new.[5] The first kind of co-operation may be helpful to the

[5] Cf. some interesting comments on evangelical attitudes to unity in a review of *The Unity and Disunity of the Church* by Geoffrey Bromiley and *Preaching on Christian Unity*, edited by Robert Tobias: 'In Bromiley there is lacking the deep sense of urgency; a sense of the "scandal of disunity". This is why the two books offer an instructive contrast. We are faced with the prospect of a union almost certain to be achieved because of the zeal of its proponents and yet doomed to judgment because it rejects the living God and his Word.

'On the other hand, we see a union which would have every prospect of being blessed and yet at present doomed to failure because those to be unified do not really want it. Is this why Bromiley's book lacks a passionate heart-beat? Perhaps it is because he has written a *treatise* in practical theology, while the liberals were *preaching sermons*. But it may well be that evangelicals, rightly or wrongly, do not have the all-consuming desire for unity which characterizes the ecumenical movement. To evangelicals it is not clear – as it seems clear to the ecumenists – that God has spoken for church union. It is just as well then that evangelicals are not rushing into union for lesser reasons, reasons which will lose their force when pressures for division come later. A permanent union for evangelicals can only come when it is consummated as a matter of duty, not of shallow, temporary expediency.' John W. Sanderson, Jr, in the *Westminster Theological Journal*, May 1959 issue.

churches; it is the second which can reach out to the world. It is not yet the "one fully committed fellowship", but it is a foretaste of that corporate life which belongs to such a fellowship. And the upbuilding of the Body of Christ has begun.'[6]

This is also a valid criticism of strictly evangelical co-operation and shows the inadequacy of any mere fellowship or council of churches. Such a fellowship may promote better relations and encourage a common witness to a restricted degree, but it makes no claim to be a visible church and completely fails to meet the ecumenical challenge or solve the problem of the much-needed reformation of the church according to Scripture.

The challenge of ecumenism to evangelicals is then not just to think of ways and arguments to oppose a particular organization or programme, but to re-think for themselves what Scripture teaches concerning the nature and unity of the Church as the body of Christ and how this unity may be implemented and applied in our modern ecclesiastical situation. Ecumenism makes an appeal to Scripture, as we have seen. Evangelicals are thus being challenged on ground which they have held to be particularly, if not exclusively, their own. Unfortunately, at the moment, ground advantage has not helped in parrying this unexpected thrust from a strongly non-evangelical force. Evangelicals have been shown to be sadly unfamiliar with the sector where the attack is being mainly directed. If the battle is not to be lost evangelicals must get rid of internal dissensions, regroup their forces, and move boldly to the offensive in the Scriptural order, inspired by the vision of a united Church pure in the truth of the Gospel.

To meet the challenge of ecumenism it will not suffice

* Mackie, op. cit., pp. 5, 6.

merely to register dissent and to offer a negative criticism. The urge towards corporate unity after the ecumenical pattern will be irresistible unless one has an even higher loyalty – the truth of the Gospel. How can we explain the desire of our Protestant leaders to unite with Eastern Orthodoxy, and, if possible, even with Rome on terms which mean the denial and abandonment of the Gospel as re-discovered at the Reformation? For, make no mistake, ecumenically-minded Protestants are seeking not merely better relationships with these communions, but eventual reunion. And the basis of their discussion of, and negotiation for, reunion is the recognition of sacerdotal theory and the acceptance of liberal theology. The price of ecumenical success is the surrender of the authority and sufficiency of Holy Scripture. But ecumenism is the effect, not the cause, of the Protestant abandonment of the Biblical Gospel. Without any Biblical anchorage, our leaders and their followers naturally feel that the quest for unity is more important than loyalty to the 'insight' of a particular section of the divided Church or to the distinctive 'witness' of any particular denomination. To charge them with disloyalty to the Protestant Reformation will make no impression on their conscience, unless it can also be shown that they are disloyal to God's truth and doing no good to the cause of true Christian unity.

In view of the positive challenge presented by the Ecumenical Movement, shall we throw in our lot with it and, at least, seek to influence it from within? Some Evangelical Protestants are disposed to do so. They are convinced that involvement need not mean compromise of the truth or subscription to unscriptural error. The case for evangelical participation is put clearly and persuasively by the Rev. A. T. Houghton, Secretary of the Bible Churchmen's Missionary Society, in his booklet *What of New Delhi?*[7] At the very outset he makes the candid admission: 'There is nothing to be gained by attempting to hide the fact that evangelicals are divided about the aim and purpose and value of the World Council of Churches and the question of Evangelical representation.'[8] In his conclusions he again draws attention to this: 'That there is a problem of Evangelical participation no one would doubt, but surely the times call for a holy boldness rather than fear, and we have a duty to our own generation, to the world at large, and to God, that we witness faithfully in accordance with those insights into the truths of God's Word which we believe have been revealed by the Holy Spirit.'[9]

The present study is offered to Evangelical Protestants, perplexed about the problem of participation in the modern Ecumenical Movement. It does not contain a detailed programme of Evangelical Church unity. There is an urgent need for evangelicals to address themselves to the teaching of Scripture concerning the Church, and to seek to apply it consistently. An examination of ecumenism highlights this need, and in one sense is incomplete without a positive alternative. Yet such a study as the present one, which deals with ecumenism as an actual institution and ideology, may be useful as a preliminary step towards this. It may help to answer the question, Is Scriptural Church unity to be worked out within the framework of the World Council of Churches and ecumenical Christianity or not?

This question is not one which can be discussed with scholarly detachment. To resist the challenge of ecumenism is to fall foul of the temper and mind of the age. It is to incur the charge of being aloof, out of touch with religious

[7] London, 1962.   [8] Op. cit., p. 7.   [9] Ibid., p. 60.

[15]

realities, and unsympathetic to the crying needs of mankind. It is to be accused of ungenerous isolationism and bigoted fundamentalism. It is to be gravely misunderstood by those who have forsaken the higher loyalty of the truth of the Gospel and the higher vision of a truly Reformed Church subjected to and ordered by the Word of God. But there are grave issues involved touching the historic evangelical Protestant faith. The Ecumenical Movement is revolutionary in thought and practice, and, as we shall seek to show, bids to become the greatest menace to the truth of the Gospel since the time of the Reformation.

2 : The objective

WITHIN THE WORLD COUNCIL OF CHURCHES THERE exists a wide diversity of opinion on practically every subject. Even concerning the general object of the Ecumenical Movement, one looks in vain for unanimity. In the minds of some, its principal aim is to provide *a means of united social and political action* to meet the predicament of our age. It is agreed that it is the aim of the Church to prepare men for the next world, but equally, it is held, is it the responsibility of the Church to prepare this world for men. Only in the discharge of this responsibility, it is said, dare the Church come forward with the gospel of salvation. Indeed the word of salvation is viewed as meaning the renewal of society as well as the renewal of the soul. The blessings of the Gospel of Christ 'include the alleviation of poverty, disease and hunger, and the creating of a true fellowship that relieves the loneliness of modern mass society. . . . The wholeness of the Gospel demands a corporate expression, since it concerns every aspect of men's lives. Healing and the relief of distress, the attack upon social abuses and reconciliation, as well as preaching, Christian fellowship and worship, are all bound together in the message that is proclaimed.'[1]

The work of the W.C.C. on behalf of refugees has perhaps received more publicity than any of its other activities. This is a noble work, deserving the appreciation and praise of all. The Report of the Committee on the Division

New Delhi Report, edited by W. A. Visser 't Hooft, London, 1962, p. 86.

[17]

of Inter-Church Aid, Refugee and World Service says: 'Through the Division the churches, according to their ability, take corporate action in dealing with people in need, whoever they are, wherever they are, and whatever their need may be. Such action includes refugee service, relief work, the meeting of emergencies through natural, political or social disasters, and aid in finding a lasting solution to the problems of poverty, disease, hunger, under-employment and unemployment.'[2]

The W.C.C. seeks to find a solution to the grave international problems which threaten the peace and very survival of the world today. The range of interest in this field can be gathered from the headings of the Report on Service, such as Nature, Science and Technology, Effects of the Technical Society and the Nuclear Arms race on human dignity, The Conflict of Cultures, The Struggle for Racial Equality, Nationalism and New Nations, and Disarmament. In the Introduction to the Report of the Committee on the Commission of the Churches on International Affairs we read: 'We speak of international affairs and the ecumenical witness to the world of nations, for Christians are called to testify to the righteous and merciful will of God, the Sovereign of men and nations. Christians have an obligation to work out and apply urgently their testimony to the problems which vex the relations of states.'[3]

Such statements indicate the concern of the W.C.C. to apply Christianity to the world and to relate it to man oppressed by social and economic problems. But this is not the principal objective of the Ecumenical Movement; *it aims at one great Church, at a visible unity of all churches.* According to the Report on Unity of the New Delhi Assembly: 'Christian unity has been the primary

[2] *New Delhi Report*, p. 230. [3] Ibid., p. 262.

concern of the Faith and Order movement from the beginning, and the vision of the one Church has become the inspiration of our ecumenical endeavour.'[4]

Referring to the Service of Holy Communion according to the Anglican form which all delegates at New Delhi who were baptized communicants of their own churches had been bidden to attend, the Rev. Kenneth Slack, the General Secretary of the British Council of Churches, writes: 'It was, in fact, the long files of communicants slowly going forward to receive their spiritual food which brought a sudden but profound sense of what we were about in the midst of our much speaking. Here was a veteran of decades of ecumenical conversation, who would only see in faith the shape of the Coming Great Church. Here were vigorous youth participants filled with a responsible but eager urgency that the barriers between separated Churches should come swiftly down.'[5] Later the same writer says of the conception of unity formulated at New Delhi: 'It departs wholly from any idea that Christian unity is a wholly "spiritual" idea, not needing in any way to be made visible to men. It departs as firmly from any idea that bodies like the World Council of Churches itself, or national councils of churches, provide through co-operation an adequate conception of unity.'[6] The New Delhi Report on Unity says: 'In the fulfilment of our missionary obedience the call to unity is seen to be imperative, the vision of one Church proclaiming one Gospel to the whole world becomes more vivid and the experience and expression of our given unity more real. There is an inescapable relation between the fulfilment of the Church's

[4] *New Delhi Report*, p. 117.
[5] *Despatch from New Delhi*, London, 1962, p. 79.
[6] Ibid., pp. 87–8.

missionary obligation and the recovery of her visible unity.'[7]

Certainly, some ecumenical leaders strongly deny that the World Council aims at becoming a World Church or Super-Church. There are those, however, who speak otherwise. Indeed, not only does the Council speak with two voices on this supremely important matter; individual leaders seem to do the same. For example, Dr Franklin Clark Fry, a prominent leader, and Chairman of the influential Central Committee of the W.C.C., said in his report at New Delhi: 'The World Council not only disavowed becoming a "super-church" at its beginning at Amsterdam; its total development since then has been the most convincing refutation of the whole notion. We who are closest to the Council are constantly baffled how any such charge can be made or any such misconception can still exist, except in critics who are deliberately self-deceived.'[8]

But we, in turn, are somewhat baffled when we discover that Dr Fry says in his foreword to the report proper of the Committee, the paperback, *Evanston to New Delhi*: 'In any case the story of a Council of Churches, however great its achievements, can never be a success story until the moment when it ceases to exist as a Council, because of the emergence in reality of the Una Sancta.' These two Latin words mean one thing only here – '*one holy Church*'.

The official W.C.C. publication, *Jesus Christ, the Light of the World*, prepared for study before the New Delhi Assembly, expresses a hope similar to Dr Fry's: 'The churches have created the World Council of Churches. They have created it so that one day they might dispense with it. The World Council of Churches lives to die. If the

[7] *New Delhi Report*, p. 121.   [8] Ibid., p. 341.

churches ever become content with it or concerned solely to perpetuate it, then they will be disobedient to the heavenly vision.'[9]

These quotations give us the solution to the apparent double-talk about the coming 'super-church' or world church. Perhaps the W.C.C. does not aspire to become the world church, but it is preparing the way for this. When its work is done, it will and must disappear as a fellowship of churches, in the creation of the one great world church.

The Rev. A. T. Houghton may add his denial, asserting that the charge 'probably arises from some enthusiastic supporters of the Ecumenical Movement who use the slogan, without any authority, "One World, one Church" as though that were both desirable and possible'.[10] The truth of the matter is that this slogan is used and enthusiastically supported by no less an authority than the W.C.C.! In the Report on Unity from New Delhi it is held to be both desirable and possible: 'The vision of one church proclaiming one Gospel to the whole world becomes more vivid and the experience and expression of our given unity more real.'[11]

Many Protestants believe that it is possible to participate in the Ecumenical Movement, while at the same time maintaining an attitude of intransigence to unreformed Rome. In his presidential address at the 1962 Assembly of the Baptist Union of Great Britain and Ireland, the Rev. W. D. Jackson strongly dissented from Lord Fisher's remark that the Roman Catholic Church is now our friend. He insisted that Baptists could not go back into the

---

[9] *Jesus Christ, the Light of the World*, p. 58.
[10] *What of New Delhi?*, p. 59.
[11] *New Delhi Report*, p. 121.

Church of Rome nor even into the Church of England. Not surprisingly, Mr Jackson's remarks were later characterized as 'unhelpful' by Archbishop Ramsey. Yet the report of his speech concludes as follows: 'The president commended the World Council of Churches and urged Baptists everywhere to join with the Baptist Union in membership.'[12] Thus many who would repudiate with warmth the allegation that they are seeking to undo the work of the Reformation are loyal supporters of the Ecumenical Movement.

Despite the denials of some, however, there seems little doubt that in the minds of most of its leaders *union with Rome is the ultimate goal* of the Ecumenical Movement. Indeed it is difficult to see how, with any degree of consistency, this can be denied. Surely, in view of the admission of the Greek Orthodox Church to the W.C.C., there is no valid reason for refusing entry to Rome. Indeed, Rome is not already in the W.C.C. chiefly because she has not yet sought membership. Courtesy visits to the Pope by leading Protestant dignitaries and frequent conferences up and down the country between Protestant ministers and Roman Catholic priests can point to only one thing – a widespread desire for reunion. The presence of Roman Catholic observers at New Delhi was hailed with great delight as an indication of Rome's change of attitude, creating hopes that soon she will join the W.C.C. Ecumenism cannot deny the Romeward trend. When Dr Henry Van Dusen, an influential leader in the W.C.C., said at New Delhi that there could be no effective world ecumenicity until the Roman Catholics were brought in,[13] he was but giving expression to what must be the desired con-

---

[12] *The Times*, London, 1 May 1962.
[13] *Christianity Today*, 22 December 1961.

summation of every truly consistent supporter of ecumenism.[14]

It is interesting to read Mr Slack's comments on the position. He, with many others, has expressed the belief that the presence of these observers marks an altered attitude on the part of Rome. 'At Evanston', he writes, 'the Archbishop of Chicago, Cardinal Stritch, within whose archdiocese the Assembly met, forbade any Roman Catholic to enter the Assembly under pain of excommunication. The only exception was if the Roman Catholic's job required him to enter. Seven years later an invitation to appoint five official observers met with a warm and ready response from the Secretariat of Unity of the Vatican. It was a dramatic change.'[15] But, no evidence has been forthcoming from the Secretariat of Unity, or from any other reliable source, of a dramatic change of Roman Catholic doctrine. The change of policy to which Mr Slack refers has no doubt been caused by the dramatic change that has come over Protestantism – even since Evanston. The Romeward trend in the W.C.C. has been stepped up greatly. In recent years Rome has won much sympathy and she has succeeded in winning over many unwary, uninstructed Protestants. A weak, deformed Protestant Church which has largely forsaken the God of her salvation has been calling to Rome 'Come over and help us'.

[14] 'The majority of ecumenists recognize that their movement cannot achieve its end without the participation of the Roman Catholic Church. The Lambeth Conference have stated this explicitly on many occasions; and Fr. Florovsky (an Eastern Orthodox priest) repeated it in August 1948 at Amsterdam: "There can be no real ecumenical cooperation, no real Christian communion and no real reunion of Christians, if Rome is not included." He said the same at Evanston.' C. Boyer, S.J., *Christian Unity and the Ecumenical Movement*, London, 1962, p. 92.

[15] *Despatch from New Delhi*, p. 47.

For instance, Dr Fisher, when Archbishop of Canterbury, declared: 'We should like to see the churches of England, Scotland, the United States and any other countries bound together in one body. If the Pope would like to come in as chairman we should all welcome him.'[16]

There is thus a dramatic recognition of the absolute necessity of Rome's presence – and, according to some, her leadership – if the world is to be saved from complete spiritual disaster. Why then should Rome not send observers to New Delhi? Why should she not send observers to observe the Romeward trend and report back on its progress? There was much to observe at New Delhi to please and encourage the Papacy. Why should not Rome in this way lend her support to a body which now seems to be doing Rome's work more effectively than she herself could ever do? Rome is too experienced and astute to mistake the signs of the times when they are moving in her favour. She knows well when to act and how to act to her own advantage. So perhaps after all there has been no dramatic change – even in the matter of sending observers – since Cardinal Stritch forbade any Roman Catholic to attend the Evanston Assembly. The observers were at New Delhi because they had a job to do – and a very important one at that – to further preparations for the take-over of a Protestantism which is rapidly facing spiritual bankruptcy and liquidation.

Rome's evaluation of the Ecumenical Movement is clear. The trends of the movement are all in the direction of return to the ancient unity in the Roman Church. Dictatorships, political and religious, are much the same. Visits of leading allied statesmen, such as Mr Neville Chamberlain, however well-intentioned, and earnest appeals for

[16] *Church Times*, 31 May 1957.

peace talks, were regarded by Hitler as signs of weakness on the part of the Allies. The Nazi leader was encouraged to go ahead with his plan to go forth conquering and to conquer. Appeasement of dictators leads to conquest, assimilation and absorption. As we know, this was averted in 1939 only by a last-minute stand against the forces of aggression. So with the Roman Catholic dictatorship.

Courtesy visits and pathetic appeals for union and peace talks are to Rome signs of the weakening of Protestant faith and resistance. 'More and more', declared Father Bernard Leeming, in a lecture to a Summer School of priests at Maynooth in Ireland, '(our separated brethren) will perceive that they need the successor of St Peter and will come to him in gradual, perhaps almost imperceptible, steps, courtesy visits merging into consultative visits, and these into acceptance of a primacy of precedence in direction and guidance.'[17] We seem to be preparing for a 'Munich' Agreement – at best a mere delaying action – which will prepare the way for the eventual destruction of Protestant resistance before the guile and might of Rome. Whether or not the Protestant churches will continue to be betrayed by their leaders, or will turn to a strong Churchillian approach towards evil before it is too late, remains to be seen.

The Roman Church sees in bodies like the World Council of Churches an admission by Protestants of the sin of their divisions and the need for some form of visible external unity; and this is but a step towards the admission of the most sinful division of all – separation from the Papacy. The voice of Dr Eugene O'Doherty, Roman Catholic Bishop of Dromore, Northern Ireland, is no voice

[17] *The Bulwark*, May 1962.

crying in the wilderness: 'It is quite clear from the existence and activities of an organization like the W.C.C. that Christians who do not share the Catholic faith are alarmed by the divisions that have sprung up among them and are anxious to get back to a common creed and a common code of morals. . . . The road to unity will be long and may be rough at times, but every single step taken on that road is a step in the right direction. Let us remember that with God nothing is impossible, and that it was our Divine Lord Himself who said, "Other sheep I have which are not of this fold. Them also I will bring and they will hear my voice and there shall be one Fold and one Shepherd." '[18]

Roman Catholics are being encouraged to work and pray that Protestants may come to see this scandal of disunity. In his Lenten Pastoral, the late Cardinal D'Alton, Roman Catholic Archbishop of Armagh, said: 'In these days, when the question of the reunion of our separated brethren is being widely discussed, we should have some knowledge of how the unity of the Church was disrupted and the issues at stake. . . . The Protestant revolt in the sixteenth century was a more serious affair, bewildering in its complexity owing to the grave difference of views amongst the Reformers themselves. However they disagreed on points of doctrine, they were of one mind in repudiating the authority of the Pope. The principle they espoused of allowing each one to interpret for himself the Scriptures, which they regarded as the sole rule of faith, has led inevitably to the multiplicity of religious bodies so much at variance with Christ's ideal of one fold and one shepherd. At the present time we should in all charity pray earnestly for our separated brethren that, enlightened

[18] Lenten Pastoral in *Irish News*, 5 March 1962.

by the Holy Spirit, they may find their way back to the one fold of Christ.'[19]

The late Pope in his Encyclical Letter, *Ad Petri Cathedram* (29 June 1959), said, 'We are well aware – and it is a great consolation to us – that among those religious bodies separated from this Seat of Peter there has recently made itself felt a movement of goodwill towards the Catholic faith and Catholic usages, together with a growing respect for the Apostolic See: the love of truth is at last proving stronger than prejudice and suspicion. We know also that almost all those who call themselves Christians, though divided from us and from one another, have held numerous meetings with a view to closer mutual relations or to reunion, and have sometimes set up some form of organization for this object. This also shows their desire for at least some degree of unity.'[20] We know the kind of unity Pope John had in mind and in his prayers. In his own words, it was 'return to union with the Apostolic See'. His appeal for such unity concludes with prayer to the Virgin Mary: 'We earnestly entreat the Blessed Virgin Mary, Queen of Peace, to whose Immaculate Heart our Predecessor of happy memory, Pius XII, consecrated the human race, to obtain for us from God, by her prayers, perfect union, and true, active and militant peace. May these blessings descend upon our children in Christ and upon all those who, while separated from us, feel moved to love the truth and to desire brotherly harmony.' Pope John, as carefully pointed out by Dr Eugene O'Callaghan, Bishop of Clogher, in his Lenten Pastoral, while expressing his hopes for Christian unity, 'made it clear that he

---

[19] *Irish News*, 5 March 1962.
[20] *Catholic Documents*, published by the Pontifical Court Club, vol. IV, no. 27.

referred to a return of the separated brethren to the Catholic Church rather than to the formation of a confederation in which there would be a shared authority'.[21]

It is clear beyond a shadow of doubt where Rome stands on this question of reunion. Reunion means return to the unity of the Roman Church. In almost every statement on the question, Protestants are called 'the separated brethren' and, if this premise be accepted, Rome is perfectly logical in her conclusion. It is for the separated brethren to come back. Cardinal D'Alton put this in forthright fashion, as we saw. The Reformation, he said, was a Protestant revolt disrupting the unity of the Church, repudiating the authority of the Pope and allowing each one to interpret for himself the Scriptures regarded as the sole rule of faith. Union will only take place, therefore, when the rebels submit, accept the authority of the Pope and abandon the authority of Scripture as the sole rule of faith together with the right of private judgment. Rome can accept nothing short of this. Today there is still only one supreme and all-embracing authority recognized by Rome – the authority of the Papacy.

To return to Rome, on Rome's terms, means the surrender of distinctive evangelical truth. But we firmly believe that evangelicalism, and it alone, has been entrusted with the truth of the Gospel, and, instead of being silenced and persuaded to take its place alongside other communions, like the Orthodox and Roman, it must boldly declare that Gospel and seek to reform the unreformed in accordance with God's Holy Word.

Between so-called 'catholics' and evangelicals there is a great gulf fixed, which can never be bridged until catholics cease to be catholics or evangelicals are no longer evan-

[21] *Irish News*, 5 March 1962.

The objective

gelical. The Roman Church to her credit knows this and says so. Pope Pius XI wrote in 1928, 'It will be opportune to expound and to reject a certain false opinion which lies at the root of that complex movement by which non-Catholics seek to bring about the union of Christian Churches. . . . They say controversies and long-standing differences, which today still keep asunder the members of the Christian family, must be entirely set aside, and from the residue of doctrines a common form of faith drawn up and proposed for belief, in the profession of which all may not only know, but also feel themselves to be brethren. If the various Churches of communities were united in some kind of universal federation, they would then be in a position to oppose resolutely and successfully the progress of irreligion. . . . They assert their readiness to treat with the Church of Rome, but on equal terms, as equals with an equal. But even if they could so treat, there seems little doubt that they would do so only on condition that no pact into which they might enter should compel them to retract those opinions which still keep them outside the one fold of Christ. This being so, it is clear that the Apostolic See can by no means take part in these assemblies, nor is it in any way lawful for Catholics to give to such enterprises their encouragement or support. If they did so, they would be giving countenance to a false Christianity quite alien to the one Church of Christ.' (Encyclical Letter on 'Fostering True Religious Unity'.)[22]

We can at least understand this position. We can appreciate the uncompromising loyalty of the Roman Church to her convictions. We sympathize with the Pope when he administers his scathing rebuke to Protestant ecumenists who wish to turn a blind eye to the doctrinal differences so

[22] *True Religious Unity*, Catholic Truth Society.

fiercely contended in the past. Rome refuses to give 'countenance to a false Christianity quite alien to the one Church of Christ'. She will never merge her traditions with the 'insights' and 'contributions' of ecumenism. 'Is it not possible that one of the denominations may be right in one matter, a second right in another matter, and a third right in yet another matter? May not all share the truth, but none possess it entirely?' So asks the Rev. F. J. Ripley, a Roman Catholic writer. He goes on: 'The answer is now clear. It is a definite "No". Christ established one visible organized Church such as we have described, with its head, bishops, priests, deacons and sacraments. He gave this Church the work of unity . . . divided Christendom is not the form of Christianity Christ taught. The plain fact is that, though Christendom may be divided, Christ's Church can never be divided. We Catholics, therefore, cannot pray for the unity of the Church in essentials; it is here already. We can pray, as we do in the Mass, for unity in spirit, in obedience, in charity, in prayers. We can, and do, pray for the unity of Christendom. We know unity does exist; we know it was given to this Church by Christ. We know we are that one Church; we know that Christendom can only be united when all the straying sheep come into the one flock ruled by the one head Christ set up on earth.'[23]

In similar vein, the Rev. Sean Kelleher of the Redemptorist House of Studies, Bangalore, India, addressing the undergraduates of Queen's University, Belfast, at the annual Academic High Mass on 29 October 1961, is reported as saying: 'It would evidently be an enormous advantage to the Christian world if all who claimed to be followers of Christ returned to true unity, under the one

[23] *Christian Unity*, Catholic Truth Society.

shepherd of the one flock. It is evident, for instance, what Anglicans and Presbyterians would gain if they returned to the Catholic fold – they would have the seven sacraments, the enlightenment of the magisterium and so on. Perhaps we do not give enough thought to the prospect of what we would gain if our separated brethren were to return to us. We must humbly admit that they have something to teach us. They will not enrich us substantially, because as Catholics we are in full possession of the truth. But they certainly will give new and deeper dimensions to our Christian lives.'[24]

According to the Roman Church the true unity has never been broken. It was given to the Church by Christ, and Rome is that one Church in which exists true unity. Rome has nothing to take or learn of an essential or substantial nature from any branch of the Protestant Church; Protestantism has nothing to give or contribute. Father Charles Boyer, Professor of Theology at the Pontifical Gregorian University in Rome, and a member of the Secretariat for Christian Unity, reaffirms the traditional Roman attitude to unity, an attitude which, he claims, is clearly understood by those outside his Church: 'Catholics know, and so do non-Catholics, that the Church of Rome cannot renounce anything which constitutes dogma or morals, and that therefore the only way to include her in reunion is to accept her whole faith. That is why Catholics maintain (and non-Catholics realize that Catholics do maintain it) that the real and true aim of the movement towards unity is the acceptance of the Catholic faith by all Christians.'[25]

It is beyond understanding how our ecumenically-minded Protestant leaders fail to see this. No doubt, some

[24] *Irish News*, 30 October 1961   [25] Boyer, op. cit., pp. 92–3.

of them do see it and are quite prepared for the great surrender.

In March 1962, Dr A. C. Craig became the first Moderator of the General Assembly of the Church of Scotland to visit the Pope. The rendering of honour to the Pope by the leader of a once great Protestant Church was a pathetic spectacle. Having succeeded in gaining entry into the Papal presence, Dr Craig presented the Pope with a stone from Lake Tiberias and a silken bookmarker decorated with ancient Celtic designs, while, in return, the Pope presented him with several Papal medals and with a volume of the Acts of the first Roman Synod, as well as with a book on the activities of the Holy See in 1961. Thus, even in the simple exchange of gifts Rome remains true to her mission, while the Protestant witness is silent. But this was true ecumenism! After his visit Dr Craig said, with a feeling of obvious satisfaction, that the Pope had referred several times to 'unity among brethren in Christ'. But we have seen what Pope John thought about the 'brethren in Christ' separated from the Holy See, and what he hoped would happen to them.

What shall we say of all these tragic events that have recently taken place in our Protestant Churches? Is it due to simple credulity, deliberate evasion, or loss of evangelical Protestant conviction? Or is it strong delusion? The Protestant Churches no longer show love of the Truth, and largely ignore, and even decry, the doctrines of salvation through Christ. We are told in Scripture that, because men receive not the love of the truth that they might be saved, for this cause God shall send them strong delusion that they should believe a lie. (2 Thess. 2: 10–11.) Is this what is taking place today?

IN AN EVALUATION OF ECUMENISM, IT IS NECESSARY to consider whether its teaching is truly Biblical and Christian. This is by no means a simple procedure since the Ecumenical Movement has no system of theology. Within the World Council of Churches a wide range of doctrinal diversity is comprehended. Yet much of the impact of the movement has been due to its idealism rather than to the practical convenience of its programme. How can such idealism be compatible with the absence of a definite body of teaching? The answer is that ecumenism has several leading principles or ideals, held by its various divergent theological schools – with the exception of the evangelicals – and reflected in its literature. With these we must now join issue.

In the first place, *ecumenism appears to be more concerned with social and political matters than with the salvation of men's souls*. A reading of the Reports from New Delhi produces this impression. The Message of the Assembly to the Churches claims that: 'There is no more urgent task for Christians than to work together for community within nations and for peace with justice and freedom with them, so that the causes of much contemporary misery may be rooted out.'[1]

The Report on Service speaks of the work of the Church in terms of Christ's redemption: 'As Christ took the form of a servant and gave Himself for the reconciliation of the whole man and the whole world, Christians are

New Delhi Report, p. 321.

called to take part in His suffering and victorious ministry as servants of the Servant-Lord. The power for service is given by the Holy Spirit who uses the Church as His instrument in manifesting the Kingdom of God and Lordship of Jesus Christ in all human relations and all social structures. Reaffirming our common Christian faith, the Third Assembly of the World Council of Churches commends to its member Churches and Christians all round the world the aspirations and needs, the sufferings and hopes of all mankind, "waiting for the manifestation of the sons of God". This Report draws particular attention to some of the aspects of the life of man in Society which call for courageous, obedient thought and action today. They include accelerated technological and social changes, racial and ethnic tensions, international relations and world peace, as well as new opportunities for Christian service in our modern world. We are called to participate in service in all these areas of the contemporary world, not because of our human ability or in order to keep up with the ways of the world, but because we accept His call to respond to His redemptive work which is active in every realm of our life. This demands the responsible participation of the whole Body of Christ throughout the world in obedience, sacrifice and solidarity with men – the indispensable marks of the Servant Church.'[2]

It is obvious that redemption and reconciliation have here a social and earthly significance; the Kingdom sought comes through the improvement of material and social conditions. The Lord's redemptive work is viewed as humanitarian, bearing no relation to His work for the deliverance of men from the wrath of God and the remission of sins. The reconciliation referred to takes place

[2] *New Delhi Report*, pp. 93–4.

between man and man, not between God and man. 'Waiting for the manifestation of the sons of God' is falsely applied to the successful outcome of this social endeavour of the Church, whereas in the Bible it refers to man's complete personal redemption and vindication before the world at the Second Coming of Christ. Ecumenism's hope is in man while the Word of God places it in Christ.

In the discussion of the draft Message of the Assembly to the Churches, 'A German Lutheran delegate wanted to see a stronger emphasis on the eschatological hope, especially for the comfort of Christians living in the most difficult situations, but Dr Bliss (Chairman) hesitated to include anything "which might seem to imply that Christians are not passionately concerned about the present life" '.[3] This delegate, Bishop Meyer (Evangelical Church in Germany), 'missed any affirmation that Jesus Christ is the light, even if God permitted an atomic holocaust to overtake the world', and without the inclusion of the eschatological hope, he held (in reply to Dr Bliss) that 'the Message would be cheaply optimistic, leaving out the promise of the Gospel which would be fulfilled however desperate the situation became'.[4]

Ecumenism's primary aim, it would seem, is to gain for men a place of security in a dangerous world. Much of the time at New Delhi was taken up with cultural, racial and international problems. Questions of peace, nuclear weapons and disarmament were given great prominence. An appeal dealing with such matters was issued to all governments and peoples from the Assembly.[5] Attempts were made to commit the W.C.C. – and, by implication, the Christian Church – to one definite viewpoint on matters

[3] *New Delhi Report*, p. 41.   [4] Ibid., pp. 317–18.
[5] Ibid., p. 280.

concerning which Christians have taken different sides in the absence of any clear word of guidance in Holy Writ. This is in line with the hope of the W.C.C. that one day, having set aside the Bible as our sole authority, together with the right of private interpretation and judgment, and having also removed all our divisions, we shall have a single united Church with the authority to speak 'ex cathedra' on all matters religious and political.

Dr Eugene Carson Blake[6] is one of the most active leaders of modern ecumenism. Preaching in Grace Cathedral, San Francisco, in December 1960, he put forward his now famous plan for the reunion of the Church. In the course of his address he said: 'Never before have so many Americans agreed that the Christian Churches, divided as they are, cannot be trusted to bring to the American people *an objective and authentic Word of God on a political issue.*'[7] But the united Church presumably would be able to bring this Word. The Church would thus be elevated to a place of equal authority with the Scriptures. What is this but the vision of a great mammoth Church possessing even greater power than the present Church of Rome? What is it but the enslavement of men to the Church, and the destruction of private judgment and individual freedom? Members would be required to hear the political pronouncements of this Church – or of its leaders – as they would hear the very Word of God itself.

Some may make the rejoinder that this is only the particular view of one man. But Dr Blake's is no lone voice; his aspiration for a world Church making authoritative

[6] Stated clerk of the General Assembly of the United Presbyterian Church, U.S.A., and chairman of the W.C.C. Committee on Programme and Finance.
[7] Italics ours.

pronouncements in political matters is echoed in the official literature of the W.C.C. In a statement adopted at New Delhi by the Assembly on the recommendation of the important Policy Reference Committee, we find this: 'It (the Committee) feels that the Council should give its member Churches spiritual and practical guidance in a Christian approach to the actual questions and problems of our day, such as materialism, secularism, peace and war, social justice, etc. The W.C.C. should certainly not wait to be pushed into critical situations, but should always take the lead and initiative in asking, "What is the command of our Lord in the present time?" At the same time, the Churches themselves should be encouraged to bring their requests in this regard before the W.C.C. While it is universally recognized that the Council is a Council of *Churches* and can only do what its member churches authorize it to do, we feel that the Council as the ecumenical conscience of the churches, should be constantly vigilant for occasions where ecumenical action is particularly desirable, and where it may call upon its members to consider such action.'[8]

The evil and the danger of such hierarchical declarations was manifested in the course of the debate on Portugal's action in Angola. A strong condemnation of Portugal and an appeal to her Government to alter her policy was passed by only two votes, 179 to 177.[9] According to Kenneth Slack, 'the real issues of division were raised in an important speech by Mr Peter Kirk, M.P. for Gravesend, who made three points: Was the mere fact that Portugal's action in Angola coincided with a meeting of the W.C.C. Assembly to lead to her impeachment, when other nations in the previous seven years had not been so arraigned?

[8] *New Delhi Report*, p. 145.　　　[9] Ibid., pp. 284–90.

Was it fair that that one nation should be charged – should there not be a number of nations in the dock with her? And was Portugal to be condemned unheard, because no representatives of that land were in the Assembly, while no condemnatory word was spoken about lands whose delegates might be embarrassed? It was on these issues that the debate really turned. Some feared the effect (on the tiny evangelical minority in Portugal) of such a statement as was proposed. Others said that Russian actions must be condemned too. Could the Assembly speak on the political rights of Angolans, while remaining silent on the millions in Europe denied self-determination?'[10] But, of course, the influential leaders of the Russian Orthodox Church by this time had taken their place in the deliberations of the W.C.C.!

This matter caused A. T. Houghton some misgivings. He comments: 'What had taken place, however, was a salutary reminder that the W.C.C. needs to exercise the utmost restraint and care in any public pronouncement on international affairs.'[11] Strong opposition to such political action by the W.C.C. came from a delegate of the German Evangelical Church in the discussions following the Report of the Committee on the Commission of the Churches on International Affairs (C.C.I.A.). He 'expressed the opinion that Christians should not meddle with questions of the policy of the day. The Assembly of the W.C.C. should not deal with politics. He criticized paragraph 24 where specially one-sided plans were recommended in such a way that the report took sides with one party in the political struggle. As to the resolution on Angola, it seemed to him that the C.C.I.A. singled out there a question where the Church had nothing to fear from the power

[10] *Despatch from New Delhi*, p. 95.   [11] *What of New Delhi?*, p. 43.
[38]

criticized, whereas in other more dangerous cases the churches remained silent. He regretted that the right of peoples to self-determination was overlooked. The millions of Europeans under foreign domination were forgotten.'[12]

That there is a social application of the Gospel we readily concede. The Gospel is not merely individual, nor is it solely concerned with saving men's souls and preparing them for heaven. Christian salvation is false if it does not affect all our relationships with other people. Paul devotes the closing chapters of his letters to the Ephesians and Colossians to exhortations concerning the expression of our salvation in home, church and daily work. Indeed, all his letters contain counsel and direction relating to true Christian behaviour towards other people. It is significant, however, that the practical parts of Ephesians and Colossians follow chapters which are profoundly theological and deal with the great redemptive work of God in Jesus Christ. In other words, before the Apostle begins to apply the Gospel he gives a thorough exposition of what the Gospel is.

Our complaint about the W.C.C. is that the vital truths of the Gospel are ignored, if not denied, and the emphasis is upon this world, and the social rather than the spiritual needs of man. A common faith is sought: a faith which will provide a common bond to inspire the humanitarian ideal. Such a faith can only be attained by the surrender of the essential redemptive purposes of the Gospel. The great verities of the Christian faith are cast out and, in the words of Pope Pius XI, we are left with a 'residue of doctrines' which bears little resemblance to the historic Christian faith. The saving content of Christianity is removed and the fragments that remain are gathered up and

[12] *New Delhi Report*, p. 279.

presented to us as the very Bread of life. The division and strife occasioned by theological discussion are regarded as irrelevant and intolerable; all our energies, it is felt, are required to meet the social evils and miseries of the day. Orthodoxy, it is urged, has been unduly preoccupied with doctrine, whereas we need a more practical faith today.

Underlying this criticism is the assumption that we have to choose between doctrine and practice. This leads, logically, to the position that if the Church is to meet the social needs of mankind, she must abandon or at least modify her doctrinal position. We maintain, on the other hand, that the Church must be concerned with both doctrine and practice; to neglect either would be fatal. But the *principal* danger today is the neglect of doctrine. Of course, Christianity insists on our duty to man, and no amount of orthodoxy of belief is an alternative or substitute for this. True orthodoxy must generate a concern for the material needs of man. But, what is more, it alone can provide an effective basis and inspiration for a just and lasting social policy. The neglect of the truths of the historic Christian faith has led to the awful spiritual decline of the modern age, and this decline will inevitably lead to a breakdown of man's fondest social and humanitarian dreams. Without the Christian conception of God and man, without the spiritual renewal of man through Christ, his noblest schemes for a better world will be shattered by material greed, jealousy and selfishness.

That this is the New Testament position is, strikingly, the verdict of J. B. Phillips, whose version of the New Testament has been so popular in recent years. Dr Phillips is not an evangelical and his view of Biblical inspiration is unsatisfactory. Even so, he clearly perceives that there are radical differences between the teaching of the New Testament Epistles and modern 'Christianity'. In his preface to *Letters to Young Churches*, he observes: 'To the writers of these letters the present life was only an incident. It was lived with a due sense of responsibility, as a preface to sharing the timeless life of God Himself. To these men this world was only a part and, because of the cumulative result of human sin, a highly infected and infectious part of God's vast created universe, seen and unseen. They trained themselves, therefore, and attempted to train others, not to give their hearts to it, nor to conform to its values, but to remember constantly that they were only temporary residents, and that their rights of citizenship were in the unseen world of Reality. Today, when all the emphasis is thrown upon making the most of this life and Christianity is only seriously considered in many quarters because of its social implications, this point of view is comparatively rarely held. Yet as we read what they have to say, we may perhaps find ourselves saying a little wistfully, "perhaps these men were right".'

A second distinctive ecumenical principle is the emphasis on sacramental unity. *Ecumenism is sacramental rather than evangelical.* This may be considered the particular emphasis of the 'Catholic' wing of the movement, just as the interest in social and political matters at the expense of doctrine is especially characteristic of Liberal Protestants. On the other hand, the Anglicans and Orthodox show a real interest in political issues and, in the same way, the Protestants in the W.C.C. have come to share in this sacramental emphasis.[13] Thus this sacramentalism is

[13] Cf. D. M. Paton: 'If Catholicism is in a way to becoming biblical, Protestantism is in a way to becoming sacramental.' *Anglicans and Unity*, London, 1962, p. 25.

not so much the contribution of one segment of the movement as definitely an *ecumenical* phenomenon.

This was very marked at New Delhi. Take, for example, the following excerpt from the Report on Unity: 'Nowhere are the divisions of our Churches more clearly evident and painful than at the Lord's Table. But the Lord's Table is one, not many. In humility the Churches must seek that one Table. We would urge the Commission on Faith and Order to continue study and consultation to help us identify and remove those barriers which now keep us from partaking together of the one bread and sharing the one cup.'[14]

The prevailing emphasis on sacramental unity gives great impetus towards the attainment of a world Church. Indeed, in many ways, the sacrament of the Lord's Supper is the real uniting force and hope in ecumenism. In consequence, the strong desire for common participation in this sacrament tends to overrule the consideration of serious differences of interpretation. Although inter-communion is a vexed subject in ecumenical circles, the stumbling-block is not the diversity of views of the Sacrament but the question of the validity of 'non-Catholic' ministries and orders.

Thus, while common participation in the Lord's Supper is held to be so vital, little attempt is made to clarify and define the doctrine of the Sacrament. One delegate at New Delhi was conscious of this when he said in the discussion of the Report on Unity that 'In his view the statement was too formalistic, because while mentioning the Creed, the Gospel, the Sacraments, the Ministry, etc., it did not sufficiently explain the substance of these terms and what is understood by them'.[15]

[14] *New Delhi Report*, p. 120.   [15] Ibid., p. 134.

Why this sacramental emphasis? It would appear that according to the W.C.C. there is something peculiar to the Eucharist, some particular bond or grace of unity imparted through it, when it is given this place of prominence. For example, in the Report on Unity, under the section 'Eucharistic Unity and Division', we find this: 'If we reversed the usual order of discussion and focussed on eucharistic action – what God does and calls us to do at the Lord's Table – rather than (first of all) on eucharistic administration – i.e. the problem of a valid ministry – we might find a clearer way to the heart of an adequate sacramental doctrine. . . . We must meet, in a responsible fashion, the rising tide of impatience amongst many young people, and indeed among many others, for more prompt and certain progress toward mutual understanding in this most central and vital experience of Christian worship and witness. The urgency of finding a way to break through the present impasse on the question of inter-communion makes it imperative that denominations and confessions undertake a new examination of their eucharistic doctrines and liturgies in the light of all these new factors introduced by the ecumenical situation.'[16] It was agreed that there are 'deeply-felt differences which centre in the word inter-communion'; that there are 'widely-varying practices' concerning the celebration of the Eucharist. Surely such differences of eucharistic doctrine and liturgy require a new examination, not just 'in the light of all these new factors introduced by the ecumenical situation', but in the light of Holy Scripture? Once more the Bible as the sole rule of faith and practice is ignored. More is said of participation in the Eucharist than of obedience to the Word of God.

[16] *New Delhi Report*, p. 128.

Thus, it is only by ignoring the Word that any hope of inter-communion can be seriously entertained. This attitude to the Sacrament is quite contrary to the New Testament. It also represents a departure from the Reformed position by Protestants in the W.C.C. The Reformers taught that the Sacrament and the Word are inseparable. The Sacrament must not be taken as a sign and seal of anything but the salvation of Christ wrought by the Spirit. It must not be used to proclaim a state of unity which does not exist. It must not be used to further a unity contrary to that unity taught in the Word and arising from a saving relationship to Christ by simple faith alone. No such unity exists between, for example, an evangelical believer and one who accepts the sacramental view of the Orthodox Church or one who believes in salvation by character and service as liberals and modernists do. There is no secret unifying power in the Sacrament; there is no such sacramental efficacy in the sacred rite. It proclaims no truth not taught in the Word. It seals and confirms the essential truth of the Word – that salvation comes through the merits of Christ and is the possession of every soul born again by the direct agency of the Holy Spirit. This was the doctrine taught by the Reformers against the errors of the Roman Church. 'It is certainly true that we get no new thing in the Sacrament, we get no other thing in the Sacrament than we get in the Word. For what more would you ask than really to receive the Son of God Himself? Your heart can neither desire nor imagine a greater gift than the Son of God, who is King of heaven and earth. Therefore I say, what new thing would you have? If you get Him, you get all things with Him. Your heart cannot imagine any new thing beyond Him. Why then is the Sacrament appointed? Not that you may get any new thing, but that you may get the same thing better than you had it in the Word.'[17]

The W.C.C. has departed from the doctrine of the Lord's Supper as held by the Reformers. But let us hold firmly, in face of the fashionable sacramentalism of today, that the Sacrament of the Lord's Supper does not teach anything or give anything which is not taught in, or given by the Word. Hear the words of that courageous spokesman of true Evangelicalism in the Church of England, the late J. C. Ryle: *'The Lord's Supper is not in its right place when it is made the first, foremost, principal, and most important thing in Christian worship.* That it is so in many quarters, we all must know. The sermon, the mode of conducting prayer, the reading of "holy Scripture", in many churches are made second to this one thing – the administration of the Lord's Supper. We may well ask, "What warrant of Scripture is there for this extravagant honour?" but we shall get no answer. There are at most but five books in the whole canon of the New Testament in which the Lord's Supper is even mentioned. About grace, faith and redemption, about the work of Christ, the work of the Spirit, and the love of the Father; about man's ruin, weakness and spiritual poverty; about justification, sanctification and holy living – about all these mighty subjects we find the inspired writers giving us line upon line, and precept upon precept. About the Lord's Supper, on the contrary, we may observe in the great bulk of the New Testament a speaking silence. Even the Epistles to Timothy and Titus, containing much instruction about a minister's

---

[17] Robert Bruce: *The Mystery of the Lord's Supper* (sermons delivered in St Giles, Edinburgh, in 1589), translated and edited by T. F. Torrance, London, 1958, pp. 63–4. These sermons remain to this day unsurpassed as an exposition of the true Reformed doctrine of the Sacrament.

duties, do not contain a word about it. This fact alone surely speaks volumes! To thrust the Lord's Supper forward, till it towers over and overrides everything else in religion is giving it a position for which there is no authority in God's Word. . . . The Lord's Supper is not in its right place, *when it is pressed upon all worshippers indiscriminately*, as a means of grace which all, as a matter of course, ought to use. Once more I ask that no one will misunderstand me. I feel as strongly as anyone, that to go to church as a worshipper, and yet not be a communicant, is to be a most inconsistent Christian, and that to be unfit for the Lord's Table is to be unfit to die. But it is one thing to teach this, and quite another to urge all men to receive the Sacrament as a matter of course, whether they are qualified to receive it or not. I should be sorry to raise a false accusation. I do not for a moment suppose that any High Church clergyman recommends, in naked language, wicked people to come to the Lord's Supper that they may be made good. But I cannot forget that from many pulpits people are constantly taught that they are born again, and have grace, by virtue of their baptism; and if they want to stir up the grace within them, and get more religion, they must use all means of grace, and specially the Lord's Supper! . . . *My own firm conviction is that the Lord's Supper should on no account be placed before Christ, and that men should always be taught to come to Christ by faith before they draw near to the Lord's Table.*'[18]

This is a clear statement of evangelical truth. It condemns the place given to the Sacrament by the W.C.C. and the indiscriminate participation of Protestants and Orthodox. We do not pass judgment on any individual in the

[18] *Knots Untied*, London, 1959, pp. 143–5. (For this and other works, reference is made to the latest edition.)

Orthodox Church or, for that matter, in the Roman Church. But the plain truth is that these Churches make the Sacrament the peculiar channel for the communication of saving grace, and all who have, by baptism, been 'regenerated' are taught to come to the Supper to receive more grace and further application of the merits of Christ towards fuller salvation. As Ryle says, 'If they want to stir up the grace within them, and get more religion, they must use all means of grace and specially the Lord's Supper.' In Ecumenism the Eucharist becomes the means for stirring up the grace of desire for unity and, therefore, every effort must be made 'to break through the present impasse on the question of inter-communion'.

The attempt is being made to secure an outward unity among those who inwardly are far removed from each other in belief; to manifest an outward unity in sheer disobedience to the Word of God and command of Christ. Such external unity is a mockery of truth and a denial of that true spiritual unity and oneness which is taught in the Word of God.

The sacramental emphasis, as mentioned earlier, is a force making for unity. It is an outstanding example of a more general trend among the nominally Reformed churches towards the acceptance of Roman Catholic doctrines and practices, especially the latter. (We might also mention the readiness of many nonconformist leaders to accept episcopacy.) The present Archbishop of Canterbury, Dr Ramsey, is perhaps the most prominent representative of this trend in England. At New Delhi Dr Ramsey spoke out against the tendency to divorce unity from the truth: 'While the world's criticism must rightly humble us, we must not on that account accept the world's conception of the matter. It is not just unity, togetherness with one another that we seek. . . . It is for unity in truth and holiness that we work and pray, for that is Christ's supernatural gift to us.'[19] On the face of it, this would seem most reassuring to evangelicals; we must remember, however, that for Dr Ramsey truth is 'Catholic' truth. He has publicly attacked 'fundamentalism', and while he is opposed to Roman exclusivism he does not oppose Romanism.

In a recent television interview, Dr Ramsey admitted that there were only two doctrines which Rome would be required to give up to bring about closer relationships with other churches: the infallibility of the Pope and the claim to be the whole Catholic Church. He is quite prepared to recognize as true the fundamental errors of Rome against which the Reformers protested long before papal infallibility was declared. He is quite prepared to recognize Rome as a true church, but not the *only* true church. Roman error, superstition and idolatry are part of the total truth. 'His writings', comments the Rev. Kenneth Slack, 'have revealed a great concern that Catholic truth, as he knows it, about the ordering of the Church's life should be preserved.'[20]

Dr Ramsey and the sacramentalists are set to establish Catholicism as the faith of ecumenism. In furtherance of this the Archbishop has spared no effort to promote unity between the Church of England and the Eastern Orthodox churches. In 1962 he visited leaders of those churches in Istanbul, Athens and Moscow in an attempt to resume talks on doctrinal matters between the Orthodox and Anglican Churches. Such talks were begun in 1931 and broken off at the outbreak of the last war. His action in a Moscow church must cause every true Protestant mingled feelings of pity, shame and indignation. According to reports, the

[19] *Despatch from New Delhi*, pp. 82–3.   [20] Ibid., p. 83.

Archbishop crossed himself frequently, joined a procession of Orthodox priests to kiss the icon of St Elijah, and knelt before a religious picture, kissing its glass case twice. What childish nonsense, astonishing superstition and rank idolatry is this! But this is Ecumenism: Dr Ramsey is one of the six Presidents of the World Council of Churches.

The political and sacramental emphases already considered are but symptoms of a radical disease in ecumenism. *Its fundamental and fatal weakness is its attitude to doctrine and theology*. The authority of the Bible is set aside in practice. As a result, doctrinal differences which were thought in the past to be a matter of life and death are blurred. The distinction between truth and error is no longer thought vital. These are serious charges and must now be substantiated.

Certainly, to accuse the World Council of Churches of altogether ignoring or discounting theology would be unjust. Liberal tendencies in that direction seem to have been checked by the 'Catholic' element in the Council. As we have seen, the Archbishop of Canterbury regrets the tendency of some to divorce unity from the truth: 'It is not just unity, togetherness with one another that we seek; and ecclesiastics have sometimes slipped into talking as if it were, isolating unity from the other notes of the Church. It is for unity in truth and holiness that we work and pray, for that is Christ's supernatural gift to us. Let that always be made clear.'[21] *'Unity will not come through compromise'*, writes John Lawrence, emphasizing the point with italics.[22] In keeping with this principle, one of the means adopted in the quest for unity has been the setting up of theological study-groups, which have borne fruit in

[21] *Despatch from New Delhi*, pp. 82–3.
[22] John Lawrence, *The Hard Facts of Unity*, London, 1961, p. 21.

a volume of literature representing great learning and hard work. The quest for unity seems inextricably bound up with the quest for an ecumenical theology.

Yet this ecumenical theology, according to one speaker at New Delhi, must not be afraid to learn from the (non-Christian) faiths of the East. In the sermon preached by a Burmese Baptist minister, the Rev. U Ba Hmyin, at the opening service, the delegates to the assembly were told: 'We must have a relevant as well as a universal theology for the nurture of Christians of both East and West.' Kenneth Slack goes on to report: 'In a bold plea for coming to grips with the Oriental way of apprehending truth, seen in "Meditation, the system of Yoga and the disciplined will", the preacher asserted that "no theology will deserve to be called 'ecumenical' in the coming days which ignores Asian structures. It may use the term 'ecumenical', but it will really be parochial and Western only."'[23]

The above statements suggest that our understanding of the Gospel must be moulded according to Eastern mysticism and ascetism. They mean that the content of the Gospel must be adjusted and interpreted in the light of the highest teaching and behaviour of heathenism. Only thus, it would appear, can we have a truly ecumenical theology. A. T. Houghton comments on this address with regret: 'He pleaded for a theology which would be better understood in an Eastern setting, where "opposites can exist together as part of the whole" in Oriental thinking. From the simple proclamation of the Gospel of reconciliation he had gone to the mystical and philosophical, and left us rather in the air.'[24]

[23] *Despatch from New Delhi*, p. 32.
[24] *What of New Delhi?*, p. 29.

Nevertheless, we feel that U Ba Hmyin was preaching a clear ecumenism. He was simply following to its logical conclusion the ecumenical conception that each section of Christendom has its own 'insight' into Truth and its own 'contribution' to make to the common pool to give us a picture of total Truth. Dealing with this conception an Editorial in *The English Churchman* made the following wise and forceful comment: 'It is this ambiguity at the very foundation of the W.C.C. which causes evangelicals so much concern. No lasting understanding can be achieved on doctrinal matters if the attempt is made to build upon the shifting sands of double meanings. Nor, we believe, is the "contribution" concept and the "insight" attitude a valid position for evangelicals to accept. We are often told today that we have a contribution to make and special insights to bring as our part of the attempt to present Truth as a whole. In all humility we cannot make the concession that this view demands. We acknowledge sadly as individuals how poor our own progress and growth in grace seems to be. We have yet far to go in the knowledge and experience of Christian things. But we cannot concede that evangelicalism in its total expression and understanding is only a "contribution" and an "insight" among other views. We believe that it is close to the teaching of God's Word, and that as far as it is consonant with Holy Scripture it is no mere segment but a faithful expression and sufficient, full-orbed system of Biblical Truth.'[25]

Dr J. I. Packer, Librarian of Latimer House, Oxford, in an address given to the Fellowship of Evangelical Churchmen on 20 March 1961, sums up this ecumenical outlook clearly in these words: It 'has popularly given rise to the idea that Christian truth has been "fragmented" by

[25] *The English Churchman*, 24 November 1961.

reason of the divisions of Christendom, into a series of isolated and partial "insights", at present scattered abroad through the various theological traditions within the Christian Church, and that what is needed is to gather them all together and construct from them a grand synthesis in which all will find a place – a sort of theological rissole, or Irish stew. The common ecumenical estimate of evangelicalism is that it is one among these many traditions, due in time to be assimilated into the larger whole.'[26]

The English Churchman's Editorial points out the doctrinal dangers involved in this conception of 'contribution' and 'insight'. One is the danger of opening the door to 'Catholic' forms of doctrine and the other is the peril of increasing liberalism. There follows this thought-provoking estimate of the ecumenical situation with a pertinent warning to the involved evangelical: 'The genius behind the W.C.C. has been liberal Protestantism. Its exponents do not accept the full inspiration and authority of the Written Word of God. They have no sure standard of reference. Thus it is only a step further to think of Christianity as a whole to be itself but an insight into an even larger Truth. It is readily agreed that Christianity is the purest, the highest, and the greatest component of the "larger Truth" yet known. Nevertheless that which is best in non-Christian religions may find a place with Christianity at length in the gradual development of a World Faith. . . . Such views are not to our knowledge officially held by the W.C.C. They are expressions of individuals. In official documents and reports of previous ecumenical conferences references to the uniqueness of Christianity have found clear expression. At the same time, however, there has been a vagueness concerning the relationship of

[26] *The English Churchman*, 7 April 1961.

Christianity to other faiths. Thus from the official W.C.C. booklet, *Evanston Speaks,* which carries the Reports of the Second Assembly of the W.C.C. in 1954, we read, "The Christian knows and believes that in Jesus Christ God has given to man the full and only-sufficient revelation of Himself. The Christian will proclaim the Gospel as God's judgment upon all human quests and questions. But in his approach to men of other faiths he will humbly acknowledge that God has not left Himself without witness. Wherever he finds light he will not try to quench it but bear witness to Jesus Christ, the true Light – the light which lighteth every man." A statement like this seems at least to leave the door open for advanced theological liberals to proclaim unscriptural views concerning the relationship of Christianity to other religions.'[27]

In this connection we may refer to that remarkable 'Festival of Faith' held in San Francisco on 19 June 1955. This was a service of prayer for peace and divine guidance to the United Nations in which members of the Buddhist, Hindu, Jewish, Moslem and Christian faiths took part. An address was given on the subject 'The United Nations and World Faith'. Perhaps most significant of all – the service was conducted by a Lutheran minister from Philadelphia, the Rev. O. Frederick Nolde, D.D., Director of the Commission of the Churches on International Affairs of the W.C.C.

The apparently syncretistic tendencies just noted lead us to enquire whether in any sense the World Council of Churches has a solid theological foundation. As its doctrinal basis it now has the following formula : 'The World Council of Churches is a fellowship of Churches which confess the Lord Jesus Christ as God and Saviour accord-

[27] *The English Churchman*, 24 November 1961.

ing to the Scriptures and therefore seek to fulfil together their common calling to the glory of the one God, Father, Son and Holy Spirit.' As a general statement of Christian belief that might be acceptable; but as a complete, detailed statement of the Christian Gospel it is most unsatisfactory. It is in fact so framed as to gain the support of the various Churches, and is thus open to different interpretations and leads to a thorough-going scepticism. Vague and insubstantial as it is, it can be accepted by both Protestant and Eastern Orthodox[28] members of the W.C.C. who can easily insert into it their own respective detailed beliefs.

Nor does the basis, so far as it goes, offer any difficulty to the Roman Catholic. It omits any reference to the way in which salvation is to be appropriated, so that both evangelical and sacramental ways of salvation can be made to fit into it without any trouble. Indeed, 'a shrewd Roman Catholic observer, Father G. H. Tavard, has written that in the basis of the W.C.C. "the door is open, in principle, to Catholic forms of doctrine"'.[29] He would have had still more reason to say this of the W.C.C. definition of the Unity, which reads: 'We believe that the unity which is both God's Will and His gift to His Church is being made visible as all in each place who are baptized into Jesus Christ and profess Him as Lord and Saviour are brought by the Holy Spirit into one fully committed fellowship, holding the one apostolic faith, preaching the one Gospel, breaking the one bread, joining in common prayer, and

[28] It must be clearly understood that the Orthodox Church, while not recognizing the authority of the Pope, is no more reformed than the Roman Church. It holds, for example, the doctrines of the Mass, Invocation of the Saints and Veneration of the Virgin. So far as our protest against Ecumenism is concerned there is no difference between Eastern Orthodoxy and Romanism.

[29] Quoted in *The English Churchman*, 24 November 1961.

having a corporate life reaching out in witness and service to all, and who at the same time are united with the whole Christian fellowship in all places and all ages in such wise that ministry and members are accepted by all, and that all can act and speak together, as occasion requires, for the tasks to which God calls His people.'[30]

Of course it is not claimed by the W.C.C. that the basis gives a complete statement of Christian belief. It is not intended as a test of orthodoxy, but is rather a minimum confession of Christian faith. Certainly this basis offers no difficulty to the 'Catholic' Churches, who hold firmly to the doctrines of the Trinity and the Deity of Christ. The late Dr J. Gresham Machen has this to say concerning minimum doctrinal requirements: 'For our part we have not much sympathy with the present widespread desire of finding some greatest common denominator which shall unite men of different Christian bodies; for such a greatest common denominator is often found to be very small indeed. Some men seem to devote most of their energies to the task of seeing how little of Christian truth they can get along with. We, however, regard it as a perilous business; we prefer, instead of seeing how little of Christian truth we can get along with, to see just how much of Christian truth we can obtain. We ought to search the Scriptures reverently and thoughtfully and pray God that He may lead us into an even fuller understanding of the truth that can make us wise unto salvation. There is no virtue whatever in ignorance, but much virtue in a knowledge of what God has revealed.'[31] Such a minimum statement as the W.C.C. basis may be enough to bind different Churches in some form of visible unity; it is quite inade-

[30] *New Delhi Report*, p. 116.
[31] J. G. Machen: *What is Faith?*, Grand Rapids, 1962, pp. 159–60.

quate to secure a unity of truth according to the Scriptures. It is a denial of the very nature of evangelical Protestant faith which proclaims the exclusive rights of the Scripture and the Saviour.

Clear, honest, logical thinking on the Christian faith is threatened by the plausible half-truths or part-truths of ecumenism. It is not what ecumenism says but what it does not say that causes alarm to those who seek to uphold the historic reformed faith. The basis of the W.C.C. may not state any error, but by its omission of certain truths it leaves the way open for error and indeed tacitly recognizes error. It does not state the whole of saving truth. The Message of the Assembly in New Delhi does exactly the same in the following extract: 'When we speak to men as Christians we must speak the truth of our faith: that there is only one way to the Father, namely Jesus Christ His Son. On that one way we are bound to meet our brother. We meet our brother Christian.'[32] That is good ecumenism. It is true that Christ is the only way to the Father – but it is not the whole of saving truth. It is also true that faith alone is the way to Christ. We look in vain through the Reports from New Delhi for the affirmation of this distinctive Reformed truth. Obviously it could not be otherwise with the recognition of the Eastern Orthodox bodies who with Roman Catholics acknowledge the Deity and Saviourhood of Christ and know no other way to the Father, but introduce numerous ecclesiastical mediators and means to receive Christ and His benefits, such as Mary and the saints, the Church and the sacraments. In spite of what some ecumenists may say, here is a convincing example of seeking unity at the expense of essential saving truth.

If the basis of the W.C.C. be thought inadequate, then

[32] *New Delhi Report*, p. 321.

the advocates of ecumenism have to hand a more comprehensive basis for their Church unity. Much is made of the fact that the three main branches of Christendom, Roman, Orthodox and Protestant, accept the great historic Creeds – the Apostles', the Nicene and the Athanasian. These Creeds are sometimes known as ecumenical because they are generally accepted. What possible reason can there be for division, it is argued, when there is agreement on the fundamental doctrines of the Christian faith?

The Apostles' Creed has gained a more cordial acceptance than the other two. 'The chief things which God has revealed are contained in the Apostles' Creed' asserts a Roman Catholic Catechism.[33] It is easy to understand why Rome holds it in special regard.[34] Although it is stated that Christ died, rose again and ascended into heaven, there is no explication of His work. Moreover, the Holy Ghost is merely mentioned in the words: 'I believe in the Holy Ghost.' Nothing is said about His work in the renewal of the soul and the gifts of faith and repentance whereby salvation is received directly by the sinner. Here is one of the 'chief things' which God has revealed which is not found in the Apostles' Creed. Its absence enables the Roman, Orthodox and Anglo-Catholic churches to give firm assent to the Creed upon which they can super-

[33] *Catechism of Christian Doctrine*, Catholic Truth Society.
[34] 'It is the doctrine of the Church of Rome, though some of the most candid and judicious Romanists have been unable to assent to it, that this creed was composed by the Apostles under the guidance of the Holy Spirit; and that, of course, it is to be regarded as possessed of the same direct divine authority as the canonical Scriptures. . . . It is not, however, possessed of any great antiquity, for it was not generally received in its present form till the very end of the fourth or the beginning of the fifth century, since which time it has been adopted as the Creed of the Roman or Western Church.' William Cunningham, *Historical Theology*, London, 1960 (reprint), I, pp. 79–80.

impose, without any difficulty, other standards of doctrine including the whole scheme of grace imparted through the Church and Sacraments.

Since the Apostles' Creed gives no light on the distinctive doctrine of the Reformation, it has an obvious attraction for ecumenically-minded Protestants who are anxious to reduce essential doctrines to a minimum in the interests of agreement and union among the Churches. The Creed essentially asks no more than the doctrinal basis of the W.C.C. It is not the first time that the Creed has appeared as the hope of minimizers and compromisers in their attempt to bring about unity at the cost of truth. As the Rev. John Macpherson reminds us: 'Repeatedly the so-called Apostles' Creed has been proposed as most fit for a general church symbol.' Concerning the adequacy of this Creed, the same writer goes on to say, 'It must be judged of according to its doctrinal sufficiency and comprehensiveness. On examination, however, we find in it no doctrine of Holy Scripture, of Divine decrees, or of Divine Providence; no statement of the doctrines of grace. It is simply a résumé of leading historical truths. The incarnation and sufferings of Christ are related, but there is no reference whatever to the purpose for which He lived and died. The existence of the Church is acknowledged, but there is no doctrine of the sacraments. Belief in the forgiveness of sins is expressed, but it is not said that this is in any way connected with the redemption wrought by Christ. The resurrection and everlasting life are confessed, but how the resurrection of the just is to be attained unto, we are not told. . . . Certainly there is no heresy in it; but, of the heresies that have actually appeared throughout the history of the Church, there are few which those adopting the Apostles' Creed as their symbol might not maintain.

[58]

As a term of communion, acceptance of so general a formulary has no meaning. It would be just as well to say, "I believe the doctrines of Scripture, interpreting these in my own fashion," as to say, "I subscribe to such a general statement of doctrine as is given in the Apostles' Creed".'[35]

The ecumenical Creeds may be excellent statements of orthodox belief so far as they go, and the two later ones admirable attempts to counteract the Arian heresy of the early centuries, which was indeed what they proposed to do; but they provide no answer to the sacerdotal heresy of Romanism, Eastern Orthodoxy and Anglo-Catholicism. They provide no information regarding the way in which the salvation wrought by Christ comes to be personally appropriated by the sinner. Of course, evangelicals may insert into this general Creed the practical subjective doctrines of the Christian Gospel; but it remains true that such doctrines are not explicitly stated, and thus the Creeds are open to a diversity of interpretation, and are quite useless as a basis or bond of unity among the Churches.

A most vigorous and decisive exposure of the Apostles' Creed as a possible bond of Church union comes from the pen of Dr William Cunningham, one of the greatest divines that Scotland has produced. In his 'magnum opus', *Historical Theology*, he writes: 'An essay was once written by a Lutheran divine, in which he exhibited in parallel columns the Lutheran, the Calvinistic, and the Popish interpretations of all the different articles in the Creed. And it certainly could not be proved that any one of them was inconsistent with the sense which the words bear, or in which they might be reasonably understood. . . . Nay, it is well known that Arians, who deny the divinity of the

[35] *Handbook on the Westminster Confession*, Edinburgh, 1882, pp. 5–6.

Son and the Holy Ghost, have no hesitation in expressing their concurrence in the Creed. . . . These considerations are quite sufficient of themselves to prove that the Apostles' Creed, as it is called, is not entitled to much respect, and is not fitted to be of much use, as a summary of the leading doctrines of Christianity. A document which may be honestly assented to by Papists and Arians, by the adherents of the great apostasy and by the opposers of the divinity of our Saviour, can be of no real utility as a directory, or as an element or bond of union among the churches of Christ. And while it is so brief and general as to be no adequate protest or protection against error, it does not contain any statement of some important truths essential to a right comprehension of the scheme of Christian doctrine and the way of salvation. It is quite true that, under the different articles of the Creed, or even under any of the earlier creeds which contained merely a brief profession of faith in the Father, the Son and the Holy Ghost, we might bring in, as many authors have done, an explanation of all the leading doctrines taught us in Scripture; but it is not the less true that they are not stated in the document itself, and that there is nothing in its words which is fitted to bring them to our notice.'[36]

It is inevitable, with the appearance of new errors and heresies, that Creeds should become enlarged and more precise. Thus the Nicene Creed is more precise than the Apostles', and is itself expanded into the Athanasian. Still more detailed are the Creeds and Confessions of the Reformation era. To ask us to be satisfied with the meagre statements of the early church as giving an adequate basis of Church union is to ask us to ignore or even to accept the errors exposed and denounced in the Reformation formu-

[36] *Historical Theology*, I, pp. 89–90.

laries. As Protestants, aware of the constant menace of Romanist error, we cannot accept anything short of the minute, precise, detailed statement of the Christian Gospel set forth clearly, accurately and scripturally in such formularies as the Westminster Confession of Faith, and, to a lesser extent, the Thirty-Nine Articles of Religion.

We must be on our guard against attempts to seek union on the basis of Creeds which non-evangelical churches value so highly. They give no safeguard against Sacerdotalism. The Creeds do not say that man is justified by faith alone. Certainly, belief in the Deity and redemption of Christ is essential, but it is not enough. Belief in the Spirit as the agent of redemption, as the One who applies this redemption to the soul, is equally necessary and important. In the day of revolt from Rome the ancient Creeds were not sufficient in themselves to form a doctrinal foundation; no more are they so in the day of return to Rome. The Word of God is the only sufficient rule of faith.

Undoubtedly, there is some agreement between evangelical Protestantism and the 'Catholic' Churches. Both Orthodox and Roman Churches teach that Christ was God in the flesh and that He died on the Cross to purchase eternal life for sinful men.[37] On such matters they are nearer the truth than many modern Protestants. Why then should there not be union between Churches which have so much fundamental truth in common? Because, as our Reformers so clearly perceived, there is a vital difference in regard to the way in which the sinner comes to receive and appropriate the benefits of Christ's Passion. 'Large and impressive as was the amount of agreement,' writes Dr

[37] 'Our Saviour suffered to atone for our sins and to purchase for us eternal life.' 'Jesus Christ is called our Redeemer, because His precious blood is the price by which we were ransomed.' *Catechism of Christian Doctrine*, Catholic Truth Society.

W. P. Paterson, 'it would be superficial to minimize the significance of the issues that were raised at the Reformation. The controversy hinged upon the question as to the means by which, and the conditions under which, the superlative blessings which are promised in the Christian religion, and which are guaranteed by the Christian idea of God, fall to be appropriated by sinful men. This is undoubtedly a religious concern of the utmost moment. The fundamental heresy is to disbelieve that there is a great salvation available, and a God who is able to make it effective, but we also go perilously and disastrously astray if we mistake the conditions under which we may claim it and make it our possession.'[38]

There can be no common cause achieved between a Church which teaches that Christ is received by faith, by the direct approach of the sinner to the Saviour, and a Church which teaches that Christ can only be received indirectly through the Church and the sacraments. The doctrines of salvation by faith alone and salvation by faith plus works are irreconcilable. It was so in Paul's day and in Luther's day. Despite the passing of the centuries, despite the claims of Ecumenism, it remains so in our day.

The grace of God is largely rejected by liberal Protestantism, by a Protestantism which refuses to accept the inspired authority and sufficiency of Holy Writ; and the grace of God is largely nullified in the 'Catholic' Churches by their tradition and ecclesiasticism. In both cases we are brought back to the slavery of the Law; man is urged to establish his own righteousness by his own obedience and good works as the ground of his acceptance with God.

Popular Ecumenical Protestantism, as we have seen, ignores the vital doctrinal differences between the various

[38] *The Rule of Faith*, p. 266.

Churches, and is greatly influenced by the Liberal belief in salvation by character or service. The 'Catholic' Churches teach salvation by works and sacraments. Paul's letter to the Galatians is at once God's convincing reply to such errors and the bastion of our evangelical freedom. Hence it has been called the 'Magna Carta of Christian liberty'. This was the letter which God used to open the eyes of Martin Luther and to give birth to the Reformation. This is the letter which must open our eyes to the error and menace of Ecumenism: the letter which must be preached in these days when Protestantism is slipping back rapidly into bondage, and the Reformation is being regarded by prominent leaders of our Churches as a mistake, or as something which perhaps served a purpose in the sixteenth century but which, in this enlightened age, is only a burden to the soul and a barrier to the Church's accomplishment of her mission in the world. If the message of Galatians convinced the Reformers of the vital truth of justification by faith alone, it is no less the message for us in this day of ecumenism and of proposed fellowship with Churches which deny this truth.

The word is clear and precise: 'If any man preach any other gospel unto you than that ye have received, let him be accursed' (Gal. 1:9). Concerning false brethren who come in privily to spy out our liberty which we have in Christ Jesus, that they might bring us into bondage, Paul declares: 'To whom we gave place by subjection, no, not for an hour; that the truth of the Gospel might continue with you' (2:5). The Eastern Orthodox Church and the Roman Catholic Church have given no indication that they intend to abandon their particular beliefs concerning the way of salvation. We recognize this and leave it to the liberal and ecumenical enthusiast to expect these Churches to unite on any other understanding. The 'Catholic' Churches seek to bring compromising Protestants into bondage, but we must not give place by subjecting ourselves to them and by sacrificing our distinctive evangelical faith.

The dangers of compromise are very real. The Apostle Peter himself was swept off his feet and led into the compromise of the truth of the Gospel by the powerful Judaizing party within the Church (Gal. 2:12). He surrendered his evangelical liberty and became entangled again with the yoke of bondage when he withdrew from eating with the Gentiles at Antioch because of those who were insisting that something else, in addition to faith in Christ, was needful for salvation – in this case, circumcision. Paul had to deal very firmly with his fellow-apostle and openly rebuked him for his departure from the faith: 'We . . . knowing that a man is not justified by the works of the law, but by the faith of Jesus Christ, even we have believed in Jesus Christ, that we might be justified by the faith of Christ, and not by the works of the law: for by the works of the law shall no flesh be justified' (2:16).

In this connection, Machen points out that, after the persecution which followed Pentecost, 'There came in the early Church a time of peace – deadly, menacing, deceptive peace, a peace more dangerous by far than the bitterest war. Many of the sect of the Pharisees came into the Church – false brethren privily brought in. They were not true Christians, because they trusted in their own works for salvation, and no man can be a Christian who does that. Yet they were Christians in name, and they tried to dominate the councils of the Church. It was a serious menace; for a moment it looked as though even Peter, true Apostle though he was at heart, was deceived. His principles were right, but, by his actions, his principles, at Antioch, for one fatal moment, were belied. But it was not God's Will that the Church should perish; and the man of the hour was there. There was one man who would not consider consequences where a great principle was at stake, who put all personal considerations resolutely aside, and refused to become unfaithful to Christ through any fear of "splitting the Church". "When I saw that they walked not uprightly", said Paul, "according to the truth of the Gospel, I said unto Peter before them all . . ." Thus was the precious salt preserved.'[39]

There are, we believe, evangelicals similarly deceived today who have allied themselves with the W.C.C. and other ecumenical interests. But this can only be done at the cost of vital Christian truth, and it deserves the same rebuke as was administered to Peter. It is wrong for evangelicals to be intimidated by non-evangelicals into joining any form of fellowship or association which would mean laying aside the evangelical witness and giving countenance to non-evangelical error.

The ecumenical estimate of evangelicalism as one of many traditions or insights cannot be sustained. It means the denial of evangelicalism. The evangelical faith makes the claim to exclusive rights relating to the understanding of the Gospel. It claims to find a complete, sufficient revelation in the Scriptures and a full, final, sufficient redemption in Christ. Thus, evangelicalism cannot, without destroying itself, make common cause with liberal and sacramental traditions.

It is important to recognize that exclusive claims are made in our Protestant confessions. Such exclusivism is the distinctive mark of historic Protestant theology. While

[39] *God Transcendent*, Grand Rapids, 1949, pp. 99–100.

the Papacy accepted the Scriptures as a rule of faith, the Reformers declared Scripture to be the *only* rule of faith. In the words of the Westminster Shorter Catechism: 'The Word of God, which is contained in the Scriptures of the Old and New Testaments, is the only rule to direct us how we may glorify and enjoy him.' Evangelicalism refuses to acknowledge the authority of the tradition of the Orthodox and Roman Churches. Concerning Christ, the Catechism says He is 'the only Redeemer of God's elect'. Salvation comes through Christ alone who has made a complete sacrifice for sin once for all, apart from man's merits or works. The evangelical faith cannot accept the numerous mediators and meritorious acts of the 'Catholic' Churches. Redemption comes *wholly* from the sovereign grace of God in Christ *alone*. The Reformers did not say the sinner is justified by faith – Rome might have said so – but by faith *alone*. This Rome would not say, nor would the Eastern Orthodox Churches say so.

'The battle of the Reformation', writes B. B. Warfield, 'was fought out under a banner on which the sole authority of Scripture was inscribed. But the principle of the sole authority of Scripture was not to the Reformation an abstract principle. What it was interested in was what is taught in Scripture; and the sole authority of Scripture meant to it the sole authority of what is taught in Scripture. This, of course, is dogma; and the dogma which the men of the Reformation found taught in Scripture above every other dogma, so much above every other dogma that in it is summed up all the teaching of Scripture, is the sole efficiency of God in salvation. This is what we call the material principle of the Reformation. It was not at first known by the name of justification by faith alone, but it was from the first passionately embraced as renunciation of all human works, and dependence on the Grace of God alone for salvation. In it the Reformation lived and moved and had its being; in a high sense of the words, it is the Reformation.'[40]

Thus the doctrines of the Reformation and Ecumenism are incompatible. Not even the subtleties of oriental thinking can devise a scheme whereby these 'opposites can exist together as part of the whole'. This is brought home to us in convincing manner by Dr Eugene Blake in the proposal for Church union already referred to.[41] In it he made an astonishingly candid repudiation of our Reformed faith: 'So long as the wording "Sola Scriptura" is required, no bridge can be made between catholic and evangelical. But it is now clear in ecumenical conversation that Protestants generally have come to recognize the right place of tradition.' Thus, for the sake of a union with unreformed churches, the vital truth that Scripture alone is the rule of faith must be abandoned.

The attainment of the 'Coming Great Church', 'proclaiming one Gospel to the whole world', and 'the recovery of visible unity' obviously implies the surrender of distinctive evangelical truth. In no other way could the Eastern and Roman churches join. The one Gospel to be preached certainly will not be the Gospel of salvation through the exclusive merits of Christ and received by faith alone. Doctrinal differences are barriers to the ecumenical goal and in the view of the W.C.C. must fearlessly be put away if unity is to be attained.

[40] *Studies in Theology*, London, 1932, p. 465.   [41] On p. 36.

4: The attraction

WITHIN THE RANKS OF THE ECUMENICAL MOVEMENT, the most influential and numerous members are either Eastern Orthodox, Anglo-Catholics or Liberal Protestants, all of whom stand for a false or defective Christianity. Yet many evangelicals have taken their place in the Ecumenical Movement. What are their main reasons for doing so? What are the main arguments and attractions for linking up with the W.C.C.? Let us examine them.

The need for Church unity, it is said, arises out of the world situation today. There are common enemies to face. Politically there is the menace of Communism, socially and economically there are the threats of war and starvation. The Churches, it is said, have failed to play their due part in these spheres. To make action effective they must come together and present a common united front. This argument is put by A. T. Houghton: 'The call of the Churches overseas in face of the strengthening of the non-Christian and materialistic forces is for a coming together of the Churches, and the getting rid of unnecessary denominational differences which have no foundation in Scripture. . . . With these aspirations we must have the utmost sympathy. . . .'[1] This suggests another factor in the modern situation which gives impetus to the movement for Christian unity – what Mr Houghton calls 'the renascent ethnic religions'. The challenge of all these forces seems to demand a closing of the ranks.

We have touched on this matter already. Co-operation

[1] *What of New Delhi?*, p. 59.

to face certain material and practical needs is one thing – the Refugee problem, for example, should engage the sympathy and attention of every Christian. But to form a great united Church with a minimum of belief – even with the intention of tackling these major problems – is another. We cannot make doctrinal sacrifices touching eternal Truth – not even for the sake of concerted action on the political and social level. The Church's first obligation is the eternal welfare and destiny of men, not the merely temporal. Greater issues than nuclear warfare, the need for disarmament, the refugee problem, the growth of population, and the like confront mankind. Eternal issues of vastly greater moment – sin, judgment to come, redemption through the blood of Christ, and the wrath of God upon the unbeliever – remain, and they demand the uncompromising attention of the Christian Church as the first priority.

What are we to say in answer to the plea that unity is necessary in face of the threat of Communism and secularism? This holds the field as one of the main arguments put forward by the Roman Catholic Church for a yielding to, and acceptance of, that unity which she claims already to have achieved. She sets herself up as the great bulwark against Communism. The truth of the matter would seem to be that, on the contrary, Roman Catholicism is the breeding ground of Communism.[2] The bondage and abuses of Orthodox and Roman Churches have provided much of the impetus behind Communism. Protestantism, through its doctrine of justification by faith, has given to the world not only spiritual freedom but, as a fruit, civil and political liberty as well. Our firm answer to Rome is that we cannot give up the Protestant doctrine of justification in order to

[2] Cf. L. Boettner: *Roman Catholicism*, Philadelphia, 1962, pp. 4–7.

embrace her bondage, which breeds the very thing we seek to destroy.

We have no warrant from God to support one evil in order to destroy another. Judah was severely rebuked by the Lord for doing exactly this – seeking help against Assyria from the old enemy Egypt. 'Woe to the rebellious children that walk to go down into Egypt, and have not asked at my mouth; to strengthen themselves in the strength of Pharaoh and to trust in the shadow of Egypt! Therefore shall the strength of Pharaoh be your shame, and the trust in the shadow of Egypt your confusion' (Isa. 30: 1–3). The leaders of Judah, in forming this alliance, were guilty of trusting in an arm of flesh instead of in the Lord (Jer. 17: 5), and also of disobeying the distinct command of the One who had delivered them out of Egypt, and who said, 'Ye shall henceforth return no more that way' (Deut. 17: 16). If, therefore, we still believe that the Reformation was of God, then to seek the help of the Church of Rome, which quite openly remains the enemy of the evangelical Protestant faith (she can do no other), to meet the threat of Communism is sheer rebellion against the Lord.

In chapter 31 of his prophecy, Isaiah continues his rebuke against those of his countrymen who were bent on going down to Egypt for help. He tells them plainly that, when the Lord shall stretch out His hand, both helper and helped shall fall, but His faithful people will be defended and preserved by the power of the Lord. He then calls for a return to the Lord and for true repentance manifested in the casting away of all idols. 'Then shall the Assyrian fall with the sword, not of a mighty man' (v. 8). So may it be in our day.

Probably the most effective of the arguments used to draw evangelicals into the Ecumenical Movement consists of *an appeal to Scripture*. The main passages upon which this is based are John 17 and Ephesians 4, particularly the prayer of John 17:21 and the exhortation of Ephesians 4:3. Ecumenism, it is claimed, is truly an endeavour after the fulfilment of the Saviour's words, 'that they all may be one'. Obviously, this argument has a greater appeal to evangelicals than have those which are stated in terms of expediency and which disparage Scripture. Arguments from Scripture are based upon ground which evangelicals accept – ground, indeed, which we tend to regard as our own.

Very often, it is true, the propaganda of the Ecumenical Movement does not lay great stress upon the teaching of the Word of God. Some of its supporters, however, do state their case – in part, at least – in terms of the Bible's teaching.[3] They claim that evangelicals, for all their boasted fidelity to the Bible, have failed to face up to the teaching of Scripture on unity. Thus, they seem to speak with great authority, and embarrass some evangelicals. One reason why evangelicals have in some cases come to accept the interpretation which ecumenism places upon John 17 and Ephesians 4 is that they have had no alternative explanation and interpretation of these portions of Scripture to offer.

Yet it is not true that evangelicals have no answer to the 'Biblical' case for ecumenism. Many expositors of Scripture have shown that, when properly understood, the texts cited give no support to ecumenism.[4] (This position is en-

[3] John Lawrence opens his book, *The Hard Facts of Unity*, by quoting John 17:21 and observes, 'The declared will of God is the only true ground for Christian unity,' p. 9.
[4] Cf. W. Hendriksen: *The Gospel of John*, London, 1959, on John 17:11, 21.

dorsed even by several liberal commentators.[5]) In a brief yet thorough treatment of the teaching of John 17 and Ephesians 4,[6] one of the foremost of living expositors, Dr D. Martyn Lloyd-Jones, presents what is both a positive exposition of the New Testament teaching on Christian unity and a critical examination, in the light of this, of modern 'ecumenical' views on unity.

For the exposition of John 17 and Ephesians 4 we follow Dr Lloyd-Jones' booklet. It is not necessary here to repeat all that he says. We would refer, however, to two crucial points in his exposition of these Scriptures. First, that it must always be borne in mind that the people for whom Christ prays and those whom Paul exhorts are a restricted group with certain definite characteristics. They believe certain truths and doctrines, and they have undergone a radical regenerating experience through the work of the Holy Spirit. This means, as Dr Lloyd-Jones observes, that universalism is ruled out. Universalism, the belief that all men, irrespective of their beliefs and conduct, will eventually be saved, has so far vitiated every professed attempt to give to ecumenism a theology 'of the Word of God'. In contrast to what it teaches, 'These people who are the subjects of the unity of which our Lord is speaking are not those who happen to have been brought up in a certain country, or who happen to belong to a given race or nation, or a particular visible church. They are those who have "received His Word", His teaching, and particularly His teaching concerning Himself. . . . The unity of which He is speaking applies only to those who receive and

---

[5] E.g. A. Plummer in *The Cambridge Bible for Schools and Colleges*; J. H. Bernard in the *International Critical Commentary*; Marcus Dods in *The Expositor's Bible*.
[6] *The Basis of Christian Unity*, D. M. Lloyd-Jones, London, 1962.

believe this word – what we would now call the gospel message.'[7]

A second characteristic of true unity as taught by our Lord and by Paul is that it is something which already exists rather than something which we have to produce. The *kind* of unity spoken of is all-important. It is a spiritual and essential unity among all those in whom God has implanted new life. It is, therefore, something which God creates – the unity of (produced by) the Spirit. When Paul urges the Ephesians to *keep* the unity of the Spirit, he does so because this unity is of such a kind that they could not *produce* it if they tried. 'That is the way in which the New Testament always puts it. The unity itself is inevitable among all those who have been quickened by the Holy Spirit out of spiritual death and given a new life in Christ Jesus. What they have to be careful about is that they do not allow anything to disrupt it or in any way to interfere with it. The emphasis is entirely upon the word *keep*.'[8] Thus, in considering church unity, we must begin with the unity which already exists. Among true believers this is a reality irrespective of the outward condition and order of the visible church. In other words, John 17 and Ephesians 4 do not refer primarily to the outward organization of the visible church.

Some supporters of the Ecumenical Movement would argue that our criticism of their programme and ideals is misdirected and unfair. In its literature, they would point out, one may discover ample evidence that the modern Ecumenical Movement recognizes both that unity is to obtain among believers and that the kind of unity God wills is essentially spiritual and organic. They feel that while evangelicals, in stressing the invisible church, have

[7] Op. cit., p. 11.   [8] Ibid., p. 25.

[73]

part of the truth, in rejecting the call to manifest this in the visible Church, they are guilty of a characteristically one-sided and defective emphasis.[9] These charges are worthy of some consideration. But, for the moment, we must concentrate upon the claim that ecumenism does in fact conceive of unity in the same way as the New Testament.

In rejecting ecumenism's concept of unity as being unscriptural, we do not deny that some of its statements appear to approach to the New Testament position. We need go no further than the New Delhi Report for evidence of this. Why, then, do we not accept them at face value? Principally because these statements must be taken in their proper context. In the case of impressive citations from the New Delhi Report, we must read them in connection with the rest of that document. In it we find no indication that doctrinal orthodoxy or personal spiritual experience are considered a prerequisite for membership in the church and so for involvement in the unity of the church. When we turn to the paragraph on *Doctrinal agreement* in the Section on Unity, far from finding reassurance in this direction, we are told that 'intellectual formulations of faith are not to be identified with faith itself'.[10] This, as we have already observed, is just a reaffirmation of one of the great errors of Liberal theology. It is a disparagement of doctrine and a denial of the necessity of right belief. The Report goes on to assert that '*koinonia* (fellowship) in

[9] 'They say that Christian unity is invisible and they point to the spiritual fellowship of Evangelical Christians which leaps across the boundaries of denominations. Is not the Keswick convention an unsurpassed demonstration of Christian unity? To this I answer "yes", but I ask whether this is all that is meant by the unity for which our Lord prayed. An invisible spiritual unity is the primary meaning of Christian unity, but this needs completion in a visible unity which is no less spiritual for being visible.' Lawrence, op. cit., p. 65.

[10] *New Delhi Report*, p. 126.

Christ is more nearly the precondition of "sound doctrine" than vice versa'.[11] Such a statement is a reversal of the Biblical order, which places belief of the truth, i.e. of doctrine, before fellowship and unity. This approach, as Dr Lloyd-Jones shows in *The Basis of Christian Unity*, is a contradiction of the whole scheme of Ephesians, the very book which ecumenism cites in its support. 'The doctrine expounded in chapters 1–3 is already the basis and the background of everything the apostle has to say about unity. He does not start with unity and then proceed to doctrine; he takes up unity because he has already laid down his doctrine.'[12]

Moreover, in spite of some of its statements, ecumenism is hopelessly at odds with the New Testament teaching on Christian unity, because of its actual practice. The policy of the World Council of Churches with regard to its membership has been to receive any and every nominally Christian church, provided it accepts in some sense satisfactory to itself the basis of the W.C.C. Among these 'churches' are some which do not believe and teach the truth, and many members who give no evidence of being partakers of the life of Christ: in other words, those who lack the essential qualifications for Christian and church unity as laid down in the New Testament. Far, then, from seeking to preserve and manifest the unity which true believers, and they alone, enjoy, ecumenism conceives of church unity in terms of the amalgamation of existing denominations or 'churches'.[13] Despite its protestations, it has pursued and is pursuing a concept of the church quite different

[11] *New Delhi Report*, p. 126.   [12] Op. cit., p. 18.
[13] It is conceived by ecumenical writers that in the process of union, the existing denominations might undergo changes in form and organization. But no one has suggested that some members of any such denomination might be ineligible to join the future united church.

from that described in the passages of Scripture to which it makes appeal. We cannot, therefore, allow the validity of its appeal to the Word of God.

Practical expediency and the commands of Scripture, especially the latter, are the arguments most commonly cited in support of ecumenism. Evangelicals, however, give another reason for supporting the movement: the W.C.C., they suggest, provides *a great opportunity for witnessing* to our evangelical convictions. Surely, they say, this is to manifest the true Christian spirit, for only in this way can we make known our testimony to those with whom we disagree.

This need is stressed by the Rev. A. T. Houghton: 'How often one meets with those who have never heard the Evangelical view on some current topic of importance to the Church, and are either ignorant of its existence, or are uninterested to enquire what Evangelicals think. Surely the place where such testimony is most urgently needed is not among convinced supporters but among those who at least will give a ready hearing to views which differ from their own, if put forward with Christian courtesy.'[14] Dr Philip Hughes makes the same point in an editorial in the *International Reformed Bulletin*: 'Those scriptural and evangelical principles which we hold sacred must not indeed be compromised. But the W.C.C. is a movement which cannot be ignored, and an attitude of aloofness and scepticism on the part of evangelicals means not only a restriction of their own influence within the wider sphere of the Church Universal, but also a withholding from the W.C.C. of that very influence which should play so vital a part in its development. . . . We have a mandate to

[14] *Evangelicals and the World Council of Churches*, London, 1962, pp. 8–9.

penetrate this world of ours. Let us ensure that we penetrate it *in depth*, in every one of its spheres, and not least in the sphere of ecumenical Christianity.'[15]

We admit that we have a certain amount of sympathy for this position. It appeals to the evangelical who has not worked out consistently the teaching of Scripture on separation from evil. On occasions, motivated by a misguided missionary zeal, evangelicals seem to have ignored those parts of the Word of God where separation from evil and error rather than propagation of truth is taught. But in certain circumstances faithful Christian witness demands that the people of God actually dissociate themselves from apostasy and error. The state of affairs in the Ecumenical Movement calls for just such a witness.

Entry into the W.C.C. on the terms stated in its doctrinal basis is in itself the denial of evangelical belief, which rests on the sole sufficiency of Scripture, Christ and faith. Affiliation with the W.C.C. implies equal safeguards for all member churches, with equal rights extended even to those with whom we disagree fundamentally. As this touches on matters of doctrine and belief, such affiliation denies the very nature of evangelical conviction. (This, of course, is not the intention of those evangelicals who follow this course.)

We may be told that we have given a false picture of the situation. According to the Toronto Statement, formulated in 1950 by the Central Committee of the W.C.C., 'Membership of the World Council does not imply that each church must regard the other member churches as churches in the true and full sense of the word. This means that a church which in the light of its own confession must regard certain teachings of another member church as

[15] October 1960 issue.

errors and heresies and certain of its practices as abuses, cannot be compelled to withdraw or hold back its views because of the churches' common membership in the World Council, but can and indeed should continue in the future to hold and express its views in their full scope.'

In accordance with the familiar law of interpretation, we must see this statement in its context, which is one of tantalizing ambiguity and compromise. Particularly in this connection is the conception of the Church unsatisfactory. While non-evangelical churches need not be recognized as churches in the true and full sense of the word, yet against that we must remember that in the basis of belief the W.C.C. is declared to be a fellowship of Churches confessing Christ as God and Saviour according to the Scriptures. A member church despite its errors and abuses is by reason of its acceptance of the W.C.C. creed still regarded as a genuine Christian church.

Not only is there ambiguity in the attitude of evangelicals in the Ecumenical Movement towards those 'churches' which hold a different view of the way of salvation. The whole concept of *witness* in the W.C.C. involves a confusion as to what witnessing is. The fundamental idea of witnessing is surely that one brings the Gospel to those who are ignorant of it. The proper sphere for witness is the world. The church is a witnessing community. Yet the argument put forward by Dr Hughes, Mr Houghton and others suggests that witness must be carried on *within* the church, not by the church. The question which naturally arises is: witness to what? Are evangelicals in the W.C.C. bringing the Gospel to unbelievers among their fellow-members? Or are they simply stressing certain aspects of the Gospel to their brethren in Christ? Upon this issue the evangelicals in the W.C.C. give us no clear answer. The tragedy is that whereas most members of the W.C.C. need the Gospel, the evangelicals who know and preach it are unable to present it with its full force because the framework and basis of the W.C.C. do not allow them as members to do so.[16]

Furthermore, this argument of participating in order to witness falls before the test of experience. Historically such attempts to make the evangelical witness known and accepted have not produced the desired result. Rather they have led to the eventual loss of the evangelical testimony. Is this a reflection on the truth or power of evangelicalism that it should come off second best in contact with other traditions? Not at all. It does, however, cast a reflection on the ecumenical attitude. It shows that such affiliation and co-operation with errorists is not prospered by God. It is disobedience to the Word of God, and God does not bless disobedience.

What happens generally in such discussions between evangelicals and others is that the evangelicals have to compromise in order to get a hearing – much more so than their opponents. This is usually done by keeping silence on the distinctive 'only' truths which evangelicalism has preserved, salvation wrought by Christ alone, received by faith alone and revealed in Scripture alone. To the mind of man the other traditions of Christendom are pleasing. They present a religion which appeals much more strongly

[16] 'Those who question and query, let alone deny, the great cardinal truths that have been accepted through the centuries do not belong to the Church, and to regard them as brethren is to betray the truth. . . . They are to be regarded as unbelievers who need to be called to repentance and acceptance of the truth as it is in Christ Jesus. To give the impression that they are Christians, with whom other Christians disagree about certain matters, is to confuse the genuine seeker and enquirer who is outside.' Lloyd-Jones, op. cit., pp. 62–3.

than the true evangelical position which says that man is wholly corrupt and without strength, depending entirely upon the Lord for his salvation. Indeed no one truly understands the doctrine of the sovereignty of God's grace in salvation without being born again of the Spirit. It is therefore not difficult to understand why the first casualty in all ecumenical discussion should be the doctrine of sovereign grace. It is obvious that no progress can be made with liberals and 'Catholics' until this *bête noire* of the Reformed faith has been given up. This is not merely a concession; it is the surrender of the main bastion of the evangelical and Reformed faith.

Hear the words of Robert Haldane as he comments on the Epistle to the Romans: 'The grand reason which induced the Apostle to declare at the outset of this Epistle that he was not ashamed of the Gospel, is a reason which applies to every age as well as to that in which Christ was first preached. His declaration implies that, while in reality there is no just cause to be ashamed of the Gospel, there is in it something which is not acceptable, and that it is generally hated and despised among men. The natural man receiveth not the things of the Spirit of God; for they are foolishness unto him. They run counter to his most fondly cherished notions of independence; they abase in the dust all the pride of his self-reliance, and, stripping him of every ground of boasting, and demanding implicit submission, they awaken all the enmity of the carnal mind. Even they who have tasted of the grace of God are liable to experience, and often to yield to, the deeply rooted and sinful feeling of being ashamed of the things of God. So prevalent is this even among Christians the most advanced, that Paul deemed it necessary to warn Timothy respecting it, whose faithfulness he so highly celebrates. "Be not thou therefore ashamed of the testimony of our Lord." In connection with this, he makes the same avowal for himself as in this passage before us, declaring at the same time the strong ground on which he rested, and was enabled to resist this temptation.'[17]

We have seen how even Peter wavered and stumbled on this very matter. The letter to the Galatians was called forth to meet the temptation and danger of surrendering the doctrine of justification by faith alone. Some had already submitted: 'I marvel that ye are so soon removed from him that called you into the grace of Christ unto another gospel: which is not another' (Gal. 1:6). There was need for Paul's exhortation, 'Stand fast therefore in the liberty wherewith Christ hath made us free, and be not entangled again with the yoke of bondage' (Gal. 5:1). There is always need – even today. Such co-operation with error as we have in ecumenism is an unequal yoke because it is a yoke contrary to the will and Word of God. Constant care and vigilance must be kept if our spiritual freedom is to be maintained. We can so easily become entangled with error. There is only one safe thing to do about an unequal yoke – to break it and to be separate (2 Cor. 6:17).

History taught us this lesson as far back as 1541 when an early attempt was made at Ratisbon to heal the breach between Rome and the Reformers. The Emperor submitted a Report on Inter-Church Relations which was to be considered and examined by three leading divines on both sides. The point at issue then, as now, was the Protestant doctrine of justification by faith alone, and from the Roman Catholic side there was an attempt to concede much to the Protestant view while subtly retaining their

[17] Robert Haldane: *Exposition of the Epistle to the Romans*, London, 1960, pp. 45–6

own. Dr James Buchanan, a former Professor of Divinity in New College, Edinburgh, in his excellent treatise *The Doctrine of Justification*, writes of the matter thus: 'Strange as it may seem, an article on Justification was agreed upon in the conference of divines – subject, however, to the approbation of the Diet – an article which was afterwards found to be satisfactory to neither party, but offensive to both; and as it throws an instructive light on the new policy which began to be adopted at that time by the adherents of Rome, and which has been pursued, more or less consistently, ever since, we may mark, *first*, the large concessions which were now made in favour of the Protestant doctrine of Justification; and, *secondly*, the careful reservation of one point, and only one, which was so ambiguously expressed as to be susceptible of different interpretations, while, according to the sense in which it was understood, it involved the whole difference between the Popish and the Protestant method of acceptance with God – between Justification by imputed, and Justification by infused or inherent, righteousness. . . . The article thus carefully concocted, and couched in ambiguous terms, was satisfactory to neither party. . . . The Elector of Saxony objected strongly to the article, and complained that "the doctrine of Justification *by faith alone*, was well-nigh buried beneath appendages and explanations".'[18]

Dr Buchanan goes on to say that one of the lessons to be learned from what occurred at the Diet of Ratisbon is that: 'It shows the possibility of appearing to concede almost everything, while one point is reserved, or wrapped up in ambiguous language, which is found afterwards sufficient to neutralize every concession, and to leave the parties as much at variance as before. It has been justly said that, in

[18] *The Doctrine of Justification*, London, 1961, pp. 145, 148.

controversies of faith, the difference between antagonist systems is often reduced to a line sharp as a razor's edge, yet on one side of that line there is God's truth and on the other a departure from it. At Ratisbon, the difference between the Popish and Protestant doctrines of Justification seemed to resolve itself into one point, and even on that point both parties held some views in common. It might seem, then, that there was no radical or irreconcilable difference between the two; and yet, when they came to explain their respective views, it was found that they were contending for two opposite methods of Justification, – the one by an inherent, the other by an imputed, righteousness, – the one by the personal obedience of the believer, the other by the vicarious obedience of Christ, – the one by the inchoate and imperfect work of the Spirit *in* men, the other by the finished work of Christ *for* them, when "He became obedient unto death, even the death of the cross". *This fact shows the utter folly of every attempt to reconcile two systems, which are radically opposed, by means of a compromise between them; and the great danger of engaging in private conferences with a view to that end.*[19] In the open field of controversy, truth, so far from being endangered, is ventilated, cleared, and defined : in the secret conclaves of divines, and the cabinets of princes, it is often smothered, or silenced. It has far less to fear from discussion, than from diplomacy. There can be no honest compromise between the Popish and the Protestant doctrine of Justification – the one is at direct variance with the other, not in respect of verbal expression merely, but in respect of their fundamental principles, – and any settlement, on the basis of mutual concession, could only be made by means of ambiguous expressions,

[19] Italics ours.

and could amount to nothing more than a hollow truce, liable to be broken by either party as soon as the subject was brought again into serious discussion. This was the abortive result of the apparent agreement at Ratisbon; it settled no question, – it satisfied no party, – and it led afterwards to much misunderstanding and mutual recrimination. "Let them go on," said Luther, referring to the schemes of those who thought that the differences between Roman Catholics and Protestants might be made up by such conferences, "we shall not envy the success of their labours: they will be the first who could ever convert the devil and reconcile him to Christ. . . . The sceptre of the Lord admits of no bending and joining; but must remain straight and unchanged, the rule of faith and practice." [20]

Sometimes, the supporters of ecumenism charge us with timidity and even cowardice. We hold back from ecumenical association with other Churches, they say, because we are afraid that our beliefs will be unable to withstand the opposition. We do not really believe in our beliefs or in the power of the God in whom we make our boast. There is a measure of truth in this charge. We *are* afraid of our beliefs. We are not afraid of the opposition, we are not afraid to witness, but we are afraid of being disobedient to the Lord. History, as we have seen – and the example of Ratisbon is only one of many – teaches us that such discussion with and co-operation with other traditions on such grounds does lead to a loss of evangelical witness and belief. And this is due to the fact that such co-operation with error is contrary to the will of God.

The situation today remains unchanged. The impression is given sometimes that an important change has taken place in the attitude of the Orthodox and Roman Churches

[20] *The Doctrine of Justification*, pp. 150–2.

towards Protestantism; actually, the situation is no different from that described by Dr Buchanan. The same irritating ambiguity is also seen in ecumenical beliefs in general, and in the W.C.C. doctrinal basis and definition of unity. There reappears today the careful reservation of one point so ambiguously expressed as to be susceptible of different interpretations and, according to the sense in which it is understood, it involves the whole difference between the Popish and Protestant method of acceptance with God. The doctrinal basis of the W.C.C. is open to this condemnation because of its omission of the doctrine as to how the sinner comes to receive the benefits of Christ's passion, viz. by faith alone. The essential minimum of the W.C.C. is but a modern version of the ingenious attempt made in the seventeenth century by Le Blanc to reduce the difference between Romanism and Protestantism to a minimum. The minimizing, compromising schemes of modern ecumenists should be firmly met with the objection of the Elector of Saxony, 'The doctrine of justification by faith alone is wellnigh buried beneath appendages and explanations.' The sacramental and evangelical teachings as to the application of the benefits of the Atonement are irreconcilable. Moreover, this objection to union with Rome has equal force with respect to Eastern Orthodoxy, which now has an influential voice in modern ecumenical discussion and activity, and to Anglo-Catholicism, whose strength in the Church of England has reached such alarming proportions.

5: The menace

THE PARTICIPATION OF EVANGELICALS IN THE ECU-
menical Movement has alarming implications. It is not
merely that the reasons given for so doing are unsatisfactory. There are positive dangers inherent in this position;
the very act of participation incurs guilt. Attention must
first be drawn to the fact of complicity in error and idolatry.

Turning to the Scriptures, we find clear teaching on this
subject in the first letter to the Corinthians. The Apostle is
dealing with the question of attendance at sacrificial feasts
in heathen temples (10:14–22). Such attendance, he
writes, is sinful, it is an act of idolatry. Those who eat of
the sacrifices are partakers of the altar, they are brought
into communion with the object of such worship, they are
held to be worshipping the God of the idolatrous altar.
'Behold Israel after the flesh: are not they which eat of
the sacrifices partakers of the altar?' (v. 18). It is important
to observe that Paul condemns the act of participation
apart from the motive or intention behind it. It would be
no defence of their conduct to say that, although participating in the sacrifices of the altar, they did not actually
believe in the object of such worship and had no thought
of becoming associated with the idolatry and blasphemy
involved. Participation brought them into communion
with demons and is forbidden. 'But I say, that the things
which the Gentiles sacrifice they sacrifice to demons and
not to God: and I would not that ye should have fellowship with demons' (v. 20).

'It was of great importance for the Corinthians', comments Charles Hodge, 'to know that it did not depend on their intention whether they came into communion with devils. The heathen did not intend to worship devils, and yet they did it; what would it avail, therefore, the reckless Corinthians, who attended the sacrificial feasts of the heathen, to say that they did not intend to worship idols? The question was not what they meant to do, but what they did; not what their intention was, but what was the import and effect of their conduct. A man need not intend to burn himself when he puts his hand into the fire; or to pollute his soul when he frequents the haunts of vice. The effect is altogether independent of his intention. This principle applies with all its force to compliance with the religious services of the heathen at the present day. Those who in pagan countries join in the religious rites of the heathen, are just as much guilty of idolatry, and are just as certainly brought into fellowship with devils, as the nominal Christians of Corinth who, although they knew an idol was nothing, and that there is but one God, yet frequented the heathen feasts. The same principle also applies to the compliance of Protestants in the religious observances of Papists. Whatever their intention may be, they worship the host if they bow down to it with the crowd who intend to adore it. By the force of the act we become one with those in whose worship we join. We constitute with them and with the objects of their worship one communion.'[1]

Here is the condemnation of ecumenism. It will not avail to say, as do some, that they support the movement with good intentions without compromising their own faith or accepting the erroneous beliefs and idolatrous practices of

[1] Charles Hodge: *Exposition of the First Epistle to the Corinthians*, London, 1959, p. 194.

certain member Churches. Participation means involvement in the guilt no matter how worthy the motive or how good the intention. The W.C.C. has brought about a state of affairs in plain disregard of this principle of Scripture. Protestants have attended services of the Orthodox Church submissively and silently, and thereby have not only consented to such idolatrous worship but, according to the Apostle, shared in it and its guilt.

The Eastern Orthodox Church is idolatrous because of its use of icons and other aids in the worship of God. True, she adheres to the doctrinal basis of the W.C.C. and confesses the Lord Jesus Christ as God and Saviour, but her manner of worshipping Him is idolatrous. It is not enough to worship the one true God; it is equally important to worship Him in the divinely-appointed way. For example, when the Israelites became impatient because of the prolonged absence of Moses upon the mount, and made the golden calf, they did not consider themselves to be idolaters. It was the Lord they intended to worship by means of the calf: it was to be a feast to the Lord (Ex. 32:5). In the words of Calvin: 'Not that the people wished to change their God, but rather to have some visible token of God's presence, in accordance with their carnal apprehension.'[2] But, though perhaps unaware of it, the Israelites were breaking the second commandment which forbade the use of images in the worship of the true God. They looked upon the use of images in the same way as Roman Catholics and Eastern Orthodox do today – a visible aid to worship God. But such a practice is as much idolatry as the worship of false gods forbidden in the first commandment. Pointing out that the second commandment forbids the

---

[2] Calvin: *Commentary on Corinthians*, Grand Rapids, 1948, vol. 1, p. 322.

use of images in divine worship, Dr Charles Hodge says:
'Idolatry consists not only in the worship of false gods but
also in the worship of the true God by images.'[3]

The reports of A. T. Houghton and Kenneth Slack, for
example, make it plain that fellowship with idolatry and
error took place at the New Delhi Assembly of the W.C.C.
Without a word of Protestant protest or evangelical witness, but with obvious recognition, and even commenda-
tion of 'Catholicism', Mr Slack tells us that at New Delhi,
'Each day was, of course, framed in worship. The evening
act of prayer was usually of a simple form rather similar to
Compline. The morning worship followed a varied pattern. On a few mornings in the middle of the Assembly
various churches held their eucharistic rites. These celebra-
tions followed the Lutheran and Orthodox liturgies, and
also, even more unusual to British worshippers, the Holy
Qurbana of the ancient Syrian Orthodox Church. Only
the Lutheran rite was open to all communicants, but all
three services provided an opportunity for any who
attended to enter into the most precious element in any
church's life, its spiritual expression in worship.'[4]

Thus, Protestants were given the opportunity, indeed
were encouraged, to attend the celebration of the eucharistic rite of the Orthodox Church – the Mass. Now what is
this but partaking in the sacrifice of the altar? Such compliance in the religious observance of the Orthodox Church
is sharing in the error and guilt of a church which denies
the sufficiency of Christ and puts church and sacrament in
place of the Saviour. It is an acknowledgment of the
sacrifice of the Mass, of the mediation of Mary and the
saints, and the other grievous errors opposed and put away

[3] *Systematic Theology*, London, 1957, vol. 3, p. 291.
[4] *Despatch from New Delhi*, p. 59.

at the Reformation – it is an acknowledgment that such practices are one way of approach to God and a form of true worship. It is disobedience to the Apostolic injunction, 'I would not that ye should have fellowship with demons' (1 Cor. 10 : 20).

What did the evangelicals at New Delhi think of all this? Referring to the united acts of worship held each day, A. T. Houghton admits that 'the representative of the Coptic Orthodox Church, after using most helpful prayers, concluded with a benediction which included a reference to the prayers on our behalf of Our Lady, the Prophets and the Apostles'.[5] He is quick to point out, however, that this was 'entirely exceptional' and the only 'jarring note struck' in these services. Mr Houghton also complains about the united Communion service held on Sunday, 26 November. 'It was announced', he says, 'as "The Order for the Administration of the Lord's Supper", which might have led one to hope that it would be a simple service in which all could join happily. Unfortunately, . . . it was marred by copes and mitres and much pomp and ceremony which detracted from the simplicity of the Lord's Supper. One would have thought that here was an occasion when the presence of hundreds of delegates from non-Anglican Protestant churches would have assured that the service was taken in a dignified and reverent way, but with the utmost simplicity in ceremonial.'[6]

It would be interesting to know whether Mr Houghton and other evangelicals followed the fourth of the guiding principles which he gives for evangelicals who are involved in the Ecumenical Movement. This principle reads : 'Involvement must entail witnessing amongst those who differ, as long as one speaks the truth in love.'[7] It is difficult

[5] *What of New Delhi?*, p. 28.   [6] Ibid., pp. 30–1.   [7] Ibid., p. 60.

to see how such a witness could have been given to the Coptic and Anglican offenders, even if evangelicals wished to do so, in view of the official position of the W.C.C. set forth in the Toronto Statement: 'No Church by virtue of its membership in the World Council is under an obligation to suppress, truncate or alter its full confession of truth . . . this means that every member church must be able to bring its full untruncated witness of the truth openly and joyfully into the Council and there give it full expression without holding anything back.' In these cases a true evangelical witness would have meant asking the Coptic and Anglo-Catholic branches of the churches to suppress what they consider truth. It would have meant denying the right of these men to give full expression to their conception of truth, without holding anything back. This is the dilemma of the ecumenically involved evangelical.

This illustrates the unrealistic character of Mr Houghton's guiding principles, which may be regarded as representative of the attitude of evangelicals in the Ecumenical Movement. The third principle states: 'Involvement must allow for the free expression of one's deepest convictions.' But, according to the Toronto statement, this must hold good for all involved – not just evangelicals. Why then should Mr Houghton take exception to the Coptic Benediction? Was this priest not giving expression to one of his deepest convictions? Was the conduct of the united Communion service not the expression of deep Anglo-Catholic convictions? Within the constitutional framework of the W.C.C. this principle means very little. It affords no right or scope for the uncompromising preaching of the evangelical Protestant faith.

Mr Houghton is anxious to commend the Eastern

Orthodox Church for maintaining silence on certain of its beliefs: 'While in the case of all the contributions made by Orthodox spokesmen in the Assembly, there was always an appeal to the New Testament, there was no suggestion that the Orthodox Churches may have developed traditions which go beyond or contradict New Testament teaching.'[8] 'One of the arguments used against association with the W.C.C. has been the presence of Orthodox Churches in the membership. Experience at New Delhi would suggest that there is more danger from member churches which are nebulous in their theology, modernistic in their outlook and opposed to any form of credal statement, than from the Orthodox Churches with all their encrusted superstition and traditionalism.'[9] May we not detect here a failure to follow his own first two guiding principles: 'Involvement must never mean compromising with the truth' and 'Involvement must never involve subscribing to unscriptural error'? While Mr Houghton admits the superstition and traditionalism of the Orthodox Churches, he claims that, so long as these churches give no suggestion that they have developed traditions which go beyond or contradict New Testament teaching, all is well. But whether or not the Orthodox Churches *suggest* it, Mr Houghton knows that in fact they do hold traditions which are a deadly threat to the souls within their fold. Is no attempt to be made to expose such error? Does such error no longer matter or make any difference if only assent is given to the doctrinal basis? This silence on the part of evangelicals may not mean assent to error, but it does mean *complicity with error*. Truth is compromised and subscription to unscriptural error occurs if no protest is raised against error.

Participation in the W.C.C. involves evangelicals in an

[8] *What of New Delhi?*, p. 37.　　　　　[9] Ibid., p. 54.

intolerable situation. *How can they proclaim their evangelical convictions and at the same time observe their ecumenical commitments?* How can they be loyal at once to the Reformed Faith and to the Toronto Statement? How can they believe that salvation comes through Christ by faith *alone*, without demanding the suppression, truncation and alteration of all non-evangelical confessions of truth? Failure to make this demand involves them in the error that goes uncondemned. Silent toleration of evil is as culpable in the sight of God as active participation.

The practice of Christ gives no precedent for evangelical participation in the Ecumenical Movement. He never sacrificed truth for unity. He did not, for instance, seek a common basis for united action with the Pharisees, although their beliefs had much in common with His own teaching, e.g. concerning Moses and the resurrection. Indeed, the Lord's disciples were taken aback by His strong denunciation of the Pharisees and their teaching. They asked, 'Knowest thou that the Pharisees were offended?' His reply is significant: 'Every plant which my heavenly Father hath not planted shall be rooted up. Let them alone; they be blind leaders of the blind – and if the blind lead the blind, both shall fall into the ditch' (Matt. 15:12–14).

False teaching must be opposed, according to Christ, as a plant which God has not planted. The particular teaching He condemned was that based upon the traditions and commandments of men. It tied up God's saving work with ritualistic and ceremonial practices. The Orthodox and Roman Churches today are in the line of Pharisaical succession. False teachers should be forsaken and 'let alone', because they deceive and destroy the souls of men. The fear of giving offence, even to those who hold high ecclesiastical office, should not silence our testimony for God's truth against the vain traditions of men. We must leave blind leaders alone as did faithful men at the time of the Reformation.

In estimating the importance of ecumenism, appearances are deceptive. The ideal of an all-embracing organic unity remains only an ideal. Even in terms of the number of church unions actually effected, the achievement hitherto is not spectacular. Yet motivating these practical negotiations is a revolutionary change of attitude. We may say that underlying the quest for unity is a new sense of unity. The churches in the ecumenical movement are not united merely by a bond of friendship. When Orthodox and Protestant, sacerdotalist, liberal and evangelical come together in the W.C.C., they do so avowedly in Christian fellowship: to all appearances they are one in Christ. If this is so, it means the end of evangelical missionary activity and of a true Protestant witness.

A most significant statement in this connection was made at New Delhi by the Ethiopian Orthodox Church: 'We are distressed by the misplaced enthusiasm evinced by some groups and bodies who call themselves Christian to draw away members of the Orthodox Church into their own folds. They seem to think that this kind of sheep-stealing is part of their legitimate missionary work. In this great Assembly, where the amalgamation of the International Missionary Council of Churches is to be effected, we want to emphasize specially the importance of taking definite steps to counteract the unchristian element in the proselytizing policies of these groups.'[10]

No matter how idolatrous or apostate the Orthodox Church may be (though few think it to be so today), yet not a

[10] *The Ecumenical Review*, January 1962.

word must be said. Obviously, it would be very wrong, not to say unnecessary, for Christians to seek to evangelize fellow-Christians. In any case, the fears of the Orthodox were groundless, for at New Delhi the evangelical witness was either silent or silenced. Kenneth Slack looks upon this as one of the great triumphs at New Delhi: 'Within the World Council of Churches the Orthodox Church had seen the word "missionary" as synonymous with "proselytizing" and feared in their turn that the search for the unity of the Church should be lost in emphasis on missionary activity. The dispelling of these fears from most of those who held them, by infinite patience with them and care in interpreting one to the other, was an admirable example of the ecumenical movement at its best.'[11] Rather, this was an admirable example of the Ecumenical Movement at its worst! We must not be deceived by this statement of the Orthodox Church or fail to see what in fact lies behind it. The unity that this Church is searching for is an ecclesiastical, sacerdotal unity in which Protestantism would disappear through absorption. To achieve this, the evangelical message based upon the Word of God must be silenced. The World Council of Churches has acquiesced in this grim betrayal of the Reformation and rejection of the Apostolic endeavour that the truth of the Gospel might continue amongst us (Gal. 2:5). It is the Protestant betrayal of Protestantism.

It comes as no great surprise to read Mr Slack's final surrender: 'Outwardly – not least because the black flowing robes of the Orthodox make them so conspicuous – this Assembly marked the moving of the Council out of what one observer rightly called "the world of the Reformation". Until now, dominance within the fellowship

[11] *Despatch from New Delhi*, p. 37.

had been with those confessions, Anglican and Protestant, which were heirs of that time, as, of course, of the preceding centuries.'[12] There is the stark truth! The W.C.C. has reached one of its objectives, an objective of modern ecumenism – the break with the Reformation. Protestantism had its day, but now in our time the power is passing to 'Catholicism' as represented in the W.C.C. by the overwhelming strength of the Orthodox Churches. And this is applauded by Protestants and considered a great step in the direction of the visible unity which will eventually, it is hoped, include the Roman Church.

The theme of the Assembly at New Delhi was 'Jesus Christ, the Light of the World'. But where, apart from the Roman Catholic Church, has that light been more obscured and practically extinguished than in the Orthodox Churches with their tradition, error and unscriptural practices? 'We wait for light, but behold obscurity; for brightness, but we walk in darkness' (Isa. 59:9). Unity has become an obsession for the sake of which no attempt must be made to preach the Gospel to the lost and bring liberty to the captives. It is more important to reach a false outward unity than to seek to bring others into that true unity which comes only by saving faith in Christ and the direct agency of the Holy Spirit. Both evangelicalism and sacerdotalism are recognized as true – at least by Protestants; Orthodox and Roman Catholic Churches have shown no sign so far of consenting to such a mockery of reason. These churches can still maintain their exclusive position behind the screen of the essential minimum of belief, and patiently await the day when a rapidly disintegrating Protestantism will be assimilated into 'Catholicism'. Ecumenical Protestantism, by its recognition of

[12] *Despatch from New Delhi*, p. 48.

churches of the 'Catholic' tradition, comes under the rebuke of the prophet Isaiah, 'Woe unto them that call evil good and good evil; that put darkness for light and light for darkness; that put bitter for sweet and sweet for bitter' (Isa. 5:20).

The Protestant Churches in the W.C.C. recognize the Christian standing of member Orthodox Churches. Their attitude to Rome shows that they recognize her also as a Christian Church, despite her errors and abuses. Ecumenism cannot consistently deny Rome this recognition when the Orthodox bodies have been admitted to the W.C.C. This recognition means, as we have argued, that salvation can come through faith or sacrament. In the W.C.C. the services and worship of the Orthodox Church provide one way to approach and hold communion with the one true and living God. This illogical position is held despite the solemn word of the Apostle, 'If by grace, then is it no more of works: otherwise grace is no more grace. But if it be of works, then is it no more grace: otherwise work is no more work' (Rom. 11:6). 'A man is justified by faith without the deeds of the law' (Rom. 3:28).

Clearly, the recognition of bodies like Eastern Orthodoxy and Rome as Christian Churches, as evidenced by confession, conference and courtesy visit, is a serious departure from the historic Protestant position. These Churches, it was firmly held, had severed themselves from Apostolic Christianity and had broken and destroyed the Word of God by their vain traditions. The Mass had replaced the simple ordinance of the Lord's Supper. Human merit and intercession had been added to the sufficient merits of the Saviour. The whole paraphernalia of tradition, ceremony and Church had destroyed the vital, distinctive doctrine of justification by faith alone.

D

By reason of her denial of the scriptural way of salvation, the Reformers believed that Rome had unchurched herself and had forfeited any right to the loyalty of men. On this ground, and on this ground alone, the Reformers believed themselves justified in separating from Rome and free from the charge of schism.

Ecumenism's attitude to the Orthodox and Roman Churches is a flat repudiation of the Reformers. It is designed to heal the division the Reformers caused. It means that the Reformation was a mistake. But the errors against which the Reformers protested and fought, and which finally led to their secession from Rome, remain in the Roman Church. Indeed, since the sixteenth century more error has been introduced, so that today there is even stronger reason for separation.

Yet, while refusing, with the Reformers, to call the Roman Church a Christian Church, we do not say that there are no true Christians within her fold. We distinguish between people and the Papacy, between souls and a system. Calvin puts it, 'Therefore, while we are unwilling simply to concede the name of Church to the Papists, we do not deny that there are churches among them. The question we raise only relates to the true and legitimate constitution of the Church, implying communion in sacred rites, which are the signs of profession and especially in doctrine. . . . We do not at all deny that churches remain under his (Antichrist's) tyranny; churches, however, which by sacrilegious impiety he has profaned, by cruel domination has oppressed, by evil and deadly doctrines like poisoned potions has corrupted and almost slain; churches where Christ lies half-buried, the Gospel is suppressed, piety is put to flight, and the worship of God almost abolished; where, in short, all things are in such disorder as to present the appearance of Babylon rather than the holy city of God. In one word, I call them churches, inasmuch as the Lord there wondrously preserves some remains of His people, though miserably torn and scattered, and inasmuch as some symbols of the Church still remain – symbols especially whose efficacy neither the craft of the devil nor human depravity can destroy. But as, on the other hand, those marks to which we ought especially to have respect in this discussion are effaced, I say that the whole body, as well as every single assembly, want the form of a legitimate Church.'[13]

Indeed, Calvin and the other leading Reformers did not hesitate to identify the Pope with Antichrist, the man of sin predicted in Scripture. Many able Protestant teachers in post-Reformation times, we must confess, have not made this identification. But they agree with the Reformers in regarding the Papacy as antichristian. While the Westminster Confession of Faith seems to make the above identification, perhaps we should give heed to the more cautious view of Dr A. A. Hodge in his Commentary on the Confession: 'The word "Antichrist" occurs in the New Testament in 1 John 2:18, 22; 4:3; 2 John 7. The coming of the "man of sin", the "son of perdition", is predicted in 2 Thess. 2:3, 4. Interpreters have differed as to whether these phrases were intended to designate a personal opponent of the Lord, or principles and systems antagonistic to Him and His cause. The authors of our Confession can hardly have intended to declare that each individual Pope of the long succession is the personal Antichrist, and they probably meant that the papal system is, in spirit, form and effect, wholly antichristian, and that it marked a defection from apostolic Christianity foreseen and foretold in Scrip-

[13] *Institutes*, London, II, 1962, pp. 313–14.

ture. All of which was true in their day, and is true in ours. We have need, however, to remember that, as the forms of evil change, and the complications of the Kingdom of Christ with that of Satan vary with the progress of events, "even now are there many Antichrists" (I John 2 : 18).'[14]

The identification of the Roman Pontiff with Antichrist may or may not be true. But it is undoubtedly true that the papal system is thoroughly antichristian and this is sufficient to justify our condemnation of the Roman Church and of all associations with her by visits to the Vatican and conferences with her priests. If we adopt the popular ecumenical view and call Rome a sister Church, then no objection to the Romeward trend is valid, separation from Rome is wrong, and the Reformers were mistaken schismatics and responsible for the most sinful division in the Christian Church. But if our evaluation of Romanism is correct, the corollary would seem to be that ecumenism is not only anti-intellectual and pragmatic, but worse than that – antichristian. By its recognition of, and association with Rome, it participates in her error and guilt. Our course is clear: 'What communion hath light with darkness? What agreement hath the temple of God with idols? Wherefore come out from among them and be ye separate, saith the Lord' (2 Cor. 6 : 14–17).

We repeat – we must 'stand fast in the liberty wherewith Christ hath made us free, and not be entangled again with the yoke of bondage' (Gal. 5 : 1). To what liberty was Paul referring? To the very liberty that modern Ecumenism threatens to destroy. *Ecumenism, as we find it in the W.C.C., would entangle us again with the yoke of bondage.* The liberty is that which comes from the Gospel of salva-

[14] *The Confession of Faith*, London, 1961, p. 319.

tion through Christ alone, apart from any works of man; the yoke of bondage is any teaching which would make the sinner dependent upon himself or upon other men for his salvation. In brief, Paul is warning us against the danger of lapsing into the belief that man can even in part earn acceptance with God. It is, therefore, a much-needed polemic to meet the climate of opinion of which Dr Martyn Lloyd-Jones speaks, that 'which dislikes anything which is really distinctive in doctrine or in life' and which 'is against any clear and precise demarcation of truth and error'.[15] We must discern the vital difference between a faith which declares that Christ and His work is *sufficient* for salvation and a faith which holds merely that Christ and His work is *necessary* for salvation. Evangelicalism is the exclusive exponent of the first, while theological liberalism and modernism on the one hand, and the sacramentalism of Orthodox and Roman Churches on the other fall into the second category.

Dr Machen puts the case with his characteristic clarity: 'What was the difference between the teaching of Paul and the teaching of the Judaizers? What was it that gave rise to the stupendous polemic of the Epistle to the Galatians? To the modern Church the difference would have seemed to be a mere theological subtlety. About many things the Judaizers were in perfect agreement with Paul. The Judaizers believed that Jesus was the Messiah; there is not a shadow of evidence that they objected to Paul's lofty view of the Person of Christ. Without the slightest doubt, they believed that Jesus had really risen from the dead. They believed, moreover, that faith in Christ was necessary to salvation. But the trouble was, they believed that something else was also necessary; they believed that what

[15] *Maintaining the Evangelical Faith Today*, London, 1959, pp. 4–5.

Christ had done needed to be pieced out by the believer's own effort to keep the Law. From the modern point of view the difference would have seemed to be very slight. Paul as well as the Judaizers believed that the keeping of the Law of God, in its deepest import, is inseparably connected with faith. The difference concerned only the logical – not even, perhaps, the temporal – order of three steps. Paul said that a man (1) first believes in Christ, (2) then is justified before God, (3) then immediately proceeds to keep God's Law. The Judaizers said that a man (1) believes on Christ and (2) keeps the Law of God the best he can, and then (3) is justified. The difference would seem to modern "practical" Christians to be a highly subtle and intangible matter, hardly worthy of consideration at all in view of the large measure of agreement in the practical realm. What a splendid cleaning-up of the Gentile cities it would have been if the Judaizers had succeeded in extending to those cities the observance of the Mosaic law, even including the unfortunate ceremonial observances! Surely Paul ought to have made common cause with teachers who were so nearly in agreement with him. Surely he ought to have applied to them the great principle of Christian unity.

'As a matter of fact, however, Paul did nothing of the kind; and only because he (and others) did nothing of the kind does the Christian Church exist today. Paul saw very clearly that the difference between the Judaizers and himself was the difference between two entirely distinct types of religion; it was the difference between a religion of merit and a religion of grace. If Christ provides only a part of our salvation, leaving us to provide the rest, then we are still hopeless under the load of sin. For no matter how small the gap which must be bridged before salvation can be attained, the awakened conscience sees clearly that our wretched attempt at goodness is insufficient even to bridge that gap. The guilty soul enters again into the hopeless reckoning with God, to determine whether we have really done our part. And thus we groan again under the old bondage of the Law. Such an attempt to piece out the work of Christ by our own merit, Paul saw clearly, is the very essence of unbelief; Christ will do everything or nothing, and the only hope is to throw ourselves unreservedly on His mercy and trust Him for all.'[16]

According to the Westminster Shorter Catechism, 'Justification is an act of God's free Grace, wherein He pardoneth all our sins, and accepteth us as righteous in His sight, only for the righteousness of Christ imputed to us, and received by faith alone'. Here we see that the ground of justification is the righteousness of Christ only, imputed to us and received by faith alone. This is directed against the Romish conception of salvation by infused righteousness. While Christ is said by Rome to be the Redeemer through His work and sacrifice, this work is not *sufficient* for man's redemption. Christ's work only merits grace for all men, such grace being received through the sacraments, enabling man to perform works which become the real ground of forgiveness. 'The condition of the sinner's acceptance with God, in short, is that he has been made righteous through the influences brought to bear upon him in the gracious economy of the Gospel. The inherent personal righteousness which has been wrought in him and the good works in which it finds expression, are properly meritorious, and merit further increments of grace, and at the last eternal life.'[17] In a word, Christ does not save anyone by His work alone: He only does something to

---

[16] *Christianity and Liberalism*, Grand Rapids, n.d., pp. 23–5.
[17] W. P. Paterson, *The Rule of Faith*, p. 255.

help men save themselves by their works or by their response to His work. Hence the Roman emphasis upon the Church and the Sacraments through which Christ's merit and grace are dispensed to enable men to do what is required to secure salvation. The evangelical believer cannot, therefore, rightly support any association with Churches that would mean the denial of the true Protestant doctrine of justification by faith without works which, Luther said, is 'the article of a standing or a falling Church'.

The rank and file of Protestantism must be warned. The ecumenical climate is depressing and soporific. It is slowly drying up our evangelical fervour. The soft winds of false doctrine are lulling us to sleep and carrying us slowly but surely in a Romeward direction. The cause of true Protestantism is at stake. The work and sacrifice of Reformers and martyrs are in danger of being brought to naught. Like Paul, let us refuse to be subjected to attempts to destroy the sufficiency of Christ for salvation; unlike Peter, in a weak moment, let us not be intimidated by the fashionable ecumenism into surrendering our Christian liberty. Better even that the Protestant Church should perish than be reunited with 'Catholic' error, superstition and idolatry. 'Flee from idolatry', the Word of God warns us (1 Cor. 10:14). Ecumenism is the new idolatry of the day. As a climate and obsession, with its efforts to achieve union at the cost of essential truth, with its pursuit of union for the sake of union, ecumenism has come between the souls of men and the God of truth. That is idolatry.

Let us give heed to the words of one of the greatest defenders of the faith, John Jewel. In his famous *Apology* (1562), generally regarded as one of the most able works of the Reformers in their controversy with Rome, he concludes, 'Neither do we eschew concord and peace, but to have peace with men we will not be at war with God. . . . Wherefore, if the Pope will have us reconciled to him, his duty is first to be reconciled to God; for as Cyprian saith, "from thence spring schisms and sects because men seek not the head and have not recourse to the fountain of the Scriptures, and keep not the rules given by the Heavenly Teacher; for that is not peace, but war; neither is he joined unto the Church, which is severed from the Gospel".'[18]

And a final judgment is in order from one who doctrinally stood in the historic Protestant succession, the late Bishop J. C. Ryle. He writes: 'Unity in the abstract is no doubt an excellent thing: but unity without truth is useless. Peace and uniformity are beautiful and valuable: but peace without the Gospel – peace based on a common Episcopacy, and not on a common faith – is a worthless peace, not deserving of the name. When Rome has repealed the decrees of Trent, and her additions to the Creed – when Rome has formally renounced image-worship, Mary-worship, and transubstantiation – then, and not till then, it will be time to talk of reunion with her. Till then there is a gulf between us which cannot be honestly bridged. Till then I call on all Christians to resist to the death this idea of reunion with Rome.'[19]

This is clear, honest, logical thinking. This is consistent, virile, Scriptural Protestantism. The call is even more urgent today. The process of 'unprotestantizing', already successfully at work in Ryle's day within the Church of England, has now developed at an alarming rate in all the major denominations. The World Council of Churches is 'unprotestantized'. It has accorded recognition to error

[18] J. Jewel, *Works*, London, 1848, III, p. 107.
[19] *Knots Untied*, p. 319.

and idolatry akin to that of Rome, in Eastern Orthodoxy. The Romeward trend is no longer a matter for denial or even debate. It is an established fact.

Let us not be deceived. The Ecumenical Movement is an affront to truth. It is a blatant repudiation of the faith of the Reformers and a shameless indictment of their action. It is a grievous offence against the God of our salvation.

Ecumenism is the enemy of the Gospel of regeneration by the Spirit and justification by faith alone. Let Evangelical Protestantism be faithful even unto death rather than enter into an allegiance with the idolatry of Orthodoxy and Romanism, and the unbelief of liberalism. The truth which promotes the glory of God must not be sacrificed for a unity which is primarily concerned with the good of man. Let Jesus Christ be praised though man and the world should perish. Let His Gospel be preached, for it is the power of God unto salvation to everyone that believes. 'The just shall live by faith.' 'Stand fast therefore in the liberty wherewith Christ hath made us free, and be not entangled again with the yoke of bondage.'

Appendix

'The Council and Reunion'

A BOOK WHICH HAS ATTRACTED GREAT ATTENTION and received much praise from both Roman Catholics and Protestants is *The Council and Reunion*,[1] by Hans Küng, Professor in the Catholic Theology Faculty of the University of Tübingen. The case for the changing, 'reformed' Roman Catholicism of today is presented candidly and forcefully. It is an excellent statement of Roman Catholic ecumenism.[2] Archbishop Lord Fisher is quoted as saying, 'You should all look at it! I have never read such a book in my life!'

The book certainly contains much to please the Protestant, and much, perhaps, that a few years ago would not have passed the censorship of the Roman Church. The author is by no means representative of all modern Roman Catholic theologians. But, from start to finish, Dr Küng shows no real understanding of the historic Protestant faith, and completely ignores the vital spiritual issue of the Reformation. Let us not be deceived by the criticisms he makes of his Church nor by the 'Catholic' reforms which he advocates. If all his criticisms were accepted and all his reforms carried out, the Roman Church would remain essentially the same.

Some of the reforms Dr Küng would like to see introduced by the Council are popular systematic Bible-reading, services conducted in the vernacular, congregational wor-

[1] Sheed and Ward, 1962.
[2] Cf. *Roman Catholics and Unity*, Enda McDonagh, London, 1962, which takes a similar position.

ship, and communion in both kinds. Let us admit that such reforms would be heartily welcomed. But even so, what difference would these make to the real vital issue at stake? None! The deadly errors of Rome would remain though practised and presented in a different form. For example, what if the people were encouraged to read the Bible so long as tradition and the right of the Church to interpret it remain, and so long as the Bible read has the words 'Do penance and be converted', which, according to Dr Küng, is the Word of the Lord to which the Church is subject?[3] What if the Mass were said in the language of the people? What difference would it make? The 'blasphemous fable' would remain, no matter how it was told.

Dr Küng proposes no change of fundamental doctrine: 'We cannot speak of any "deformation" in the Church's dogma, such as is possible in theology, nor in consequence, in this sense, of a "reform" of doctrine.'[4] He is attempting merely to clear away abuses and additions which stand in the way of gaining Protestant acceptance of Roman dogma.

He does, however, urge reform of doctrine in one sense. But this does not mean that any doctrine comes to be cast aside as untrue. Reform of doctrine means a more complete statement of already existing unchanging truth: 'What the Catholic Church does recognize in her dogma is the giving of new forms or more developed forms to a doctrine which has not in every respect achieved its complete form; as the Vatican Council defined it, a growth and advance. . . . There is a *development* of dogma, in the sense of an unfolding of what is implicit so as to make it explicit, under the influence of the Holy Spirit. Although dogmatic definitions express the truth with infallible accuracy and are in this sense unalterable (as against

[3] *The Council and Reunion*, p. 50.   [4] Ibid., p. 162.

Modernism), yet they are by no means rigid, fossilized formulae. . . . One and the same truth of faith can always be expressed in a still more complete, more adequate, better formula. Thus a truth that is, as it were, wrapped up in the particular historical outlook of one age can be set free from it and placed in a wider, more adequate (but still finite) historical perspective.'[5] Thus Rome cannot reform her beliefs, in the Protestant sense of the word. Catholic reform means a development or an unfolding of what is already there. It, therefore, means to the Protestant *a growth or advance in error*. Roman truth never changes, although it may become more explicit and more complete, and may be expressed in a more adequate manner. But the new formula expresses 'the same truth of faith'. Thus Roman truth can never be shown to be false or less true; it can only be shown to be more true.

Dr Küng is advocating merely a new expression and presentation of old Roman errors in liturgy, ceremony and discipline. He speaks of 'a reform of the Mass' but, strictly, this means a reform of 'the liturgy of the Mass'. The language may be changed, the manner of celebration may be reformed, but the Mass itself remains: 'The Catholic Church herself could reap marvellous blessings from such a reform of the Mass. There would be a huge increase in the intelligibility and popular character of the Mass.'[6] He deplores abuses of the cult of Mary and the saints, but not the cult itself. He agrees with one Doctor of the Church who, while zealously defending the veneration of Mary, also said: 'We recognize that things have crept into the cult of Mary, which disfigure it. . . . There are some fanatics who have grown crazy enough to practise superstition and idolatry instead of the true cult, and to forget

[5] *The Council and Reunion*, pp. 162–4.   [6] Ibid., p. 259.

all proper limits, in respect both of God and of Mary.'[7] 'Protestants can then', he says, 'be sure that we too realize the dangers, and this not only in northern countries. No pleasure is taken at Rome in the mounting number of reports of apparitions, and the pseudo-apparitions at Heroldsbach are enough to show that the authorities are prepared to act.' This is all to the good, but again it leaves the vital issue untouched. We object not to any mere disfigurement of the cult of Mary but to the cult itself, the aim of which is to bring 'souls to Jesus by the speediest, most total and most loving transformation possible of the old man into the new man of righteousness and Christian holiness' (Cardinal Montini, now Pope Paul VI, quoted).[8] Thus the Marian cult is a denial of the Protestant doctrine that not Mary but faith brings souls to Jesus.

It is of the greatest importance for Protestants to know what Rome claims to teach concerning the place and power of secondary mediators, such as Mary and the saints. She affirms that Christ is the only Mediator between God and man. Let us make no ill-informed false accusation on this matter, as many Protestants do. Dr Ludwig Ott writes in *Fundamentals of Catholic Dogma*:[9] 'The title Co-redemptress must not be conceived in the sense of an equation of the efficacy of Mary with the redemptive activity of Christ, the sole Redeemer of humanity (1 Tim. 2:5) . . . Mary merited the application of the redemptive grace of Christ. In this manner she co-operates in the subjective redemption of mankind. . . . According to God's positive ordinance, the redemptive grace of Christ is conferred on nobody without the actual intercessory co-operation of Mary.'

---

[7] *The Council and Reunion*, p. 184.   [8] Ibid., pp. 185, 186.
[9] Cork, 1958 (most recent English edition), pp. 212–13.

The Roman Church carefully avoids making Mary or the saints share with Christ in the *purchase* of redemption. Her deadly error is in making them share in the *application* of redemption, which means the denial of the sufficiency of Christ's work for the *effectual* redemption of the soul. No matter how Rome may claim to believe that Christ is the one and only Mediator between God and man, she, in effect, destroys His Saviourhood by introducing numerous mediators, Mary and the saints, between Christ and man. The cult of Mary is therefore quite incompatible with the Gospel as understood by Protestants, that the sinner can approach the Saviour personally and directly, and, by simple faith alone, appropriate the redemption of Christ.

The Mass – ignoring for the moment its most objectionable feature as a propitiatory sacrifice, the implications of which Rome tries to evade – also takes the place of faith when it is regarded as the means of appropriating the benefits of Christ's Passion. 'The sacrifice of the Mass', says Dr Ott, 'is the means whereby the fruits of the sacrifice of the Cross are applied to mankind in need of salvation.' There is no indication given by Dr Küng or any other exponent of Roman Catholic ecumenism that the Roman Church would ever give up these offending articles of belief in favour of union on some agreed ecumenical minimum of belief, such as we have in the doctrinal basis of the W.C.C., with a view to meeting the needs of the age. 'All too often', writes Dr Küng, 'those undertaking a "reform of doctrine" have been those who thought themselves called to give a new form to the Christian revelation, according to their own needs and prejudices and without reference to any Church or tradition, so as to formulate, in accord with the spirit of the times, some sort of incorrupt "essence of Christianity". Reform of doctrine

[113]

in this case means, in practice, a *selection* from the totality of Revelation; which is, precisely, heresy.'[10] It is thus not difficult to understand why the Roman Church has refused to join the World Council of Churches.

According to this book, reform for the Catholic is not the same as reform for the Protestant. For the Catholic it applies to change in minor matters, liturgical, ritualistic and disciplinary, or to confirmation and completion of truth; for the Protestant it means nothing short of the surrender of the vital truth which constitutes the *raison d'être* of the Reformation. In characteristic fashion Protestantism is brushed aside as false. It is taken for granted that the Reformation was an unfortunate mistake. It is admitted that the Roman Church must have some blame for the Protestant 'schism'.[11] But we must not be misled by this admission. It is not an admission of the truth of Protestant belief or of the error of Roman belief. It is simply the admission that in some ways the Roman Church was to blame for the Protestant *error*, and can today, in certain ways, help Protestants to get back to the truth which they forsook in the sixteenth century. Dr Küng is calling for a reform of the Reformation which is, in fact, a reversal of the Reformation.

In substantiation of this criticism, let us consider the following passages. What, according to Dr Küng, was the actual reason for the Roman Church's rejection of Luther? Because Luther 'brought the very essence of the Catholic Church into question when (this was the real innovation) he set his personal subjective and yet (by his intention) universally binding interpretation of the Scriptures *in principle* above the Church and her tradition'.[12]

---

[10] *The Council and Reunion*, pp. 161, 162.   [11] Ibid., p. 103.
[12] Ibid., p. 106.

What is his evaluation of the Council of Trent? He describes it as 'an epoch-making, universal expression of the Church's reform of herself from within, rooted in the central core of Catholicism'.[13] If Trent is an expression of the Church's reform from within which, according to Dr Küng, is to be Rome's contribution to reunion today, then we know that Rome will remain Rome in spite of it all.

He goes on to say: 'The decree on justification, which is the glory of the Council, accepts what is valid in the Reformers' position to a surprising degree.' The 'glory of the Council' is in fact its incisive condemnation of the Protestant doctrine of justification. Trent anathematizes (1) those who say that the ungodly man is justified by faith alone (Canon IX), (2) those who say that trust in Christ is the sole cause of justification (Canon XII), (3) those who say that justification is complete when the sinner trusts in Christ (Canon XXIV), (4) those who say that good works do not merit justification, increase of grace, eternal life and an increase of glory (Canon XXXII). Whatever the Council accepts as valid in the Reformers' position, it certainly does not accept the Reformers' Gospel.

Dr Küng believes that Rome possesses the whole of essential truth. 'Converts do not bring with them', he says, 'anything of the fundamental essential substance of truth which the Church did not have before.'[14] 'Despite all her numerous deficiencies she preserves the wholeness of Christianity, with the apostolic and Petrine succession, in a way that other communions, lacking the apostolic or Petrine succession, despite all the good there is in them, do not.'[15] In the united Church envisaged by our author,

[13] *The Council and Reunion*, p. 112. [14] Ibid., p. 134. [15] Ibid., p. 136.

the apostolic succession and papal authority must remain.

Finally, he thinks of reunion as a going over to Rome because the separated brethren can only find the fulfilment of salvation in the Roman Church. 'The Pope does not simply want individuals to come over; he wants the reunion of our separated Christian communions.'[16] He quotes from Cardinal Doepfner: 'We want our Christian brethren to be able to sense that their longing for Christ's justifying grace, entirely the work of the Holy Spirit, whose presence in them we discern and reverence, finds its full scope and indeed its fulfilment, within the Catholic Church.'[17]

This could be an extremely dangerous book. It will, understandably, make a strong appeal to the undiscerning and to those who hold the popular diluted Protestantism of today. The hero of the book is the late Pope John XXIII. In answer to the question, How can Catholics and Protestants come together again? Dr Küng replies: 'The right way is the way on which John XXIII has set out.'[18] That way was clearly put forth in the Pope's first Encyclical *Ad Petri Cathedram*, 29 June 1959, where, 'in a spirit of earnest affection', he called upon the separated brethren 'to return to union with the Apostolic See'. Dr Küng's call to his Church to self-criticism and renewal will, almost certainly, promote and hasten, by enticing words of man's wisdom, the fulfilment of the hope entertained by the Vatican.

All possible steps should be taken to dispel the fears of Protestants, and lead them to acknowledge the right and authority of the Petrine office: 'Can the Protestant Christian who is a man of good will hear, from the Chair of Peter as it is today, the *voice of the Good Shepherd*? . . .

[16] *The Council and Reunion*, p. 137. [17] Ibid., p. 139. [18] Ibid., p. 133.

We Catholics can hear that voice, and we give thanks to Christ, who is the Lord of our Church, that we can hear it: the voice of Christ through the voice of him who, during the time of His absence, is to shepherd the flock. But if there is ever to be unity over this most difficult of questions, the question of the Pope, then we Catholics must get to know and try to understand the questionings and doubts, the objections and difficulties that Protestants make against the primacy as it is today. And we must try on our side – once more in an honest attempt at self-criticism and self-reform – to do our best and utmost to enable not only ourselves who are within the Church's walls, but the millions outside to hear the voice of the Good Shepherd.'[19] We need not be deceived. To help the cause of unity, Catholics must try to understand the questionings and difficulties of Protestants concerning the Pope. But why? *To remove the difficulties, not the Pope!* All Catholic discussion and self-reform, as we have already seen, has one aim in view – to secure the return of Protestants to union with the Papal See. Cardinal Liénart, Archbishop of Lille, in his Introductory Message to the French edition of the book, is frank about this: 'There are many Christians of all communions who long for that unity which Jesus Christ willed, and who place in the coming Council their hopes that a way may be opened to it. They will be happy to find out from this book how the Catholic Church, as she works for her own renewal throughout, can make a useful contribution to helping on the return to unity, in a common adherence to "the truth which makes free".'

How far has Dr Küng succeeded in his aim? The back cover of the second edition of his book bears the comment of the *Church of England Newspaper*: 'It is

[19] *The Council and Reunion*, pp. 205–6.

certainly a work in a million. . . . The cause of reunion will substantially advance if this little work becomes a best-seller. Most readers will, I think, avow with Lord Fisher that they have never read a book like it in their lives.' Suffice it to say that it *has* become a best-seller.

Some other Banner of Truth Trust publications

Ecumenism and the Bible. DAVID HEDEGARD

If the nineteenth century was the century of missionary expansion, the movement for church unity has been the distinctive ecclesiastical development of the present century. In a spate of books, the ecumenical movement has been considered from almost every conceivable angle. *Ecumenism and the Bible*, as its title suggests, is one of the few to examine the history and teachings of ecumenism specifically in the light of the Bible.

The author, a distinguished evangelical leader in Sweden, was for some years lecturer in New Testament Introduction at the University of Lund. This book was first published in 1953 in Sweden and provoked wide discussion. It has been carefully revised for a new English edition. In addition, two completely new chapters have been added – on *Evangelical Missions in the Age of Ecumenism* and *The Second Vatican Council*.

Dr Hedegard is unable to share in the general optimism as to the outcome of the ecumenical movement. His conclusions are unlikely to be popular. They are, however, worthy of serious consideration, being documented from the ecumenical and theological literature of several countries. We believe that this book makes a real and much-needed contribution to the subject.

240 pp.   4s. 6d.

*Systematic Theology. LOUIS BERKHOF

Professor Berkhof died in 1957, at the age of 83. He was an outstanding American teacher and the author of some twenty-two books. After two pastorates, he began his long career as professor at Calvin Seminary, Grand Rapids, in 1906. Here he remained for thirty-eight years, devoting his talents and immense stores of knowledge to the training of men for the ministry. His *Systematic Theology* was his *magnum opus*, being revised and enlarged during his lifetime until it reached its present final form.

Berkhof's loyalty to the well-defined lines of the Reformed Faith, his concise and compact style and his up-to-date treatment have made this work the most important twentieth-century compendium of Reformed Theology.

'The work seemed particularly important to me,' writes the author, 'in view of the widespread doctrinal indifference of the present day, of the resulting superficiality and confusion in the minds of many professing Christians, of the insidious errors that are zealously propagated even from the pulpits, and of the alarming increase of all kinds of sects. If there ever was a time when the Church ought to guard her precious heritage, the deposit of the truth that was entrusted to her care, that time is now.'

784 pp.   30s.

* As editions of titles thus marked are available from American publishers, readers will understand that we are unable to export copies of our English editions to the U.S.A. or Canada.

Lectures on Revivals. WILLIAM B. SPRAGUE

The subject of revival has become almost fashionable today. There is general agreement amongst Evangelicals that we need a revival. But there are many views as to what revival really is, how it may be promoted and what are the hindrances to it. Clear, scriptural and sanctified thinking and teaching on the subject is greatly needed.

This in the opinion of competent judges is just what Sprague provides. 'I consider Dr Sprague's volume', wrote John Angell James, the distinguished nonconformist leader of the last century, 'as the most important and satisfactory testimony that has yet reached us on the subject of revivals.' Charles Simeon, leader of the Evangelical party in the Church of England, inscribed in the flyleaf of his own copy, 'A most valuable book. I love the good sense of Dr Sprague.' Sprague's lectures ask and answer the questions which perplex us about revivals, as well as some which we are not, but should be, asking.

The volume is enhanced by the inclusion of letters to the author from twenty eminent American ministers, describing their own experiences of revivals and giving sound practical advice. Sprague, like them, is never dry or merely theoretical, because he lived at a time when the church in North America was being watered by the dew of heaven. The great object of his book was 'to vindicate and advance the cause of *genuine* revivals of religion'. All who have the same cause at heart may profit by reading this neglected volume.

472 pp. 15s.

The Life of Elijah. A. W. PINK

The life of Elijah has gripped the thought and imagination of preachers and writers in all ages. His sudden appearance out of complete obscurity, his dramatic interventions in the national history of Israel, his miracles, his departure from earth in a chariot of fire, all serve to that end. 'He comes in like a tempest, who went out like a whirlwind,' says Bishop Hall; 'the first that we hear from him is an oath and a threat.' Judgment and mercy were mingled throughout Elijah's astonishing career. From the moment when he steps forth, 'without father, without mother', 'as if he had been a son of the earth', to the day when his mantle fell from him and he crossed the river of death without tasting death, he exercised a ministry only paralleled by that of Moses, his companion of the Mount of Transfiguration.

It is fitting that the lessons which may be drawn from Elijah's ministry should be presented afresh to our generation. History repeats itself. The wickedness and idolatry rampant in Ahab's reign live on in our gross twentieth century's profanities and corruptions. Our lot is cast in a time of widespread and deep departure from the ancient landmarks of the people of the Lord. Truths dear to our evangelical forefathers have been trodden as the mire of the streets.

A. W. Pink's study of Elijah is particularly suited to the needs of the present day. He clearly felt called to the task of smiting the ungodliness of the age with the rod of God's anger. With this object he undertakes the exposition of Elijah's ministry and applies it to the contemporary situation. He shows that the ancient challenge, 'Where is the Lord God of Elijah?', is no mere rhetorical question. Where indeed? Are our aspirations expressed in the words of Josiah Conder?

> *Lord, with this grace our hearts inspire,*
> *Answer our sacrifice with fire*
> *And by thy mighty acts declare*
> *Thou art the God who heareth prayer.*

320 pp.

6s.

The Mystery of Providence. JOHN FLAVEL

Do we believe that everything in the world and in our own lives down to the minutest detail is ordered by the providence of God? Do we ever take time to observe and meditate on the workings of providence? If not, are we missing much? The Puritans, among others, would tell us we are.

It should be a delight and pleasure to us to discern how God works all things in the world for His own glory and His people's good. But it should be an even greater pleasure to observe the particular designs of providence in our own lives. 'O what a world of rarities', says John Flavel, 'are to be found in providence. . . . With what profound wisdom, infinite tenderness and incessant vigilance it has managed all that concerns us from first to last.' It was to persuade Christians of the excellency of observing and meditating upon this that Flavel first published his *Mystery of Providence* in 1678. Since then the work has gone through a number of editions and the Trust has published a paperback edition, slightly modernised in language and layout.

Based on the words 'God that performeth all things for me' (Ps. 57: 2) this work shows us how providence works for us in every stage and experience of our lives. The book is richly illustrated from the lives of believers and from the author's wide reading in church history. There are avenues of spiritual knowledge and experience opened to the Christian in this work which he probably never knew existed.

224 pp.   4s. 6d.

The Geneva Series of Commentaries

Psalms: David Dickson. 1056 pp., 21s.

Ecclesiastes: Charles Bridges. 336 pp., 10s. 6d.

The Song of Solomon: George Burrowes. 456 pp., 10s. 6d.

Zechariah: T. V. Moore. 250 pp., 9s.

Haggai and Malachi: T. V. Moore. 180 pp., 7s. 6d.

Mark: J. A. Alexander. 468 pp., 13s. 6d.

*John: William Hendriksen. 768 pp., 25s.

Acts: J. A. Alexander. 992 pp., 25s.

Romans: Robert Haldane. 660 pp., 21s.

*I Corinthians: Charles Hodge. 400 pp., 15s.

*II Corinthians: Charles Hodge. 320 pp., 12s. 6d.

*Philippians: William Hendriksen, 224 pp., 15s.

*I and II Timothy and Titus: William Hendriksen. 408 pp., 21s.

Hebrews: John Brown. 740 pp., 25s.

*James: Thomas Manton. 482 pp., 15s.

Jude: Thomas Manton. 378 pp., 13s. 6d.

Other Titles

Paperbacks

Adolphe Monod's Farewell		128 pp.	2s. 6d.
Brownlow North – His Life and Work	K. Moody-Stuart	224 pp.	3s. 6d.
Five Christian Leaders	J. C. Ryle	192 pp.	4s. 6d.
Five English Reformers	J. C. Ryle	160 pp.	2s. 6d.
The Gospel in Genesis	Henry Law	192 pp.	3s.
Heaven on Earth	Thomas Brooks	320 pp.	5s.
Letters of John Newton		192 pp.	2s. 6d.
A Lifting Up for the Downcast	William Bridge	288 pp.	5s.
The Life of M'Cheyne	Andrew Bonar	192 pp.	3s. 6d.
*Redemption Accomplished and Applied	John Murray	192 pp.	3s.
The Reformation in England	J. H. Merle d'Aubigné		
	Vol. 1	498 pp.	7s. 6d.
	Vol. 2	524 pp.	7s. 6d.
The Rich Man and Lazarus	Brownlow North	128 pp.	3s. 6d.
The Life of Robert Bruce	D. C. MacNicol	224 pp.	2s. 6d.
Sermons of the Great Ejection (1662)		224 pp.	3s. 6d.
Sermons of M'Cheyne		192 pp.	3s.
The Sovereignty of God	A. W. Pink	160 pp.	2s. 6d.
*A Summary of Christian Doctrine	Louis Berkhof	192 pp.	3s. 6d.
The Work of the Holy Spirit	Octavius Winslow	224 pp.	3s.

For free illustrated catalogue write to:

THE BANNER OF TRUTH TRUST
78b Chiltern Street, London, W.1